Both Sides of the Coin

Heather Mavis Owen

xulon
PRESS

Both Sides of the Coin
by Heather Mavis Owen

Printed in the United States of America

ISBN 9781625099778

www.xulonpress.com

David & Heather Owen in 1994

ROSES

These lovely flowers!
Did God make them or man?
I cannot tell
Until I smell
The perfumed petals and I feel
The velvet texture with my hand.

No thorn grows on the artificial flower
It looks so real
Yet can no fragrance give
It does not live!
Some day, 'twill fade and go back to the earth.

The real rose dies, but in due course
Will bloom again, year after year
Thus have a lasting worth.
Give me the real rose, I have no fear,
The thorns I can endure,
There's life and fragrance here!

Editor's Choice
2006 International Society of Poets.

ISAIAH 59:19

Lift up a standard against him Lord

When the enemy comes in like a flood

And stem the tides of iniquity

By the Spirit and the Word and the Blood.

We'll lift our hands and see the foe retreat

Let not your people ever know defeat

We'll shout the victory and repeat

"Lift up a standard Lord"

REVIVAL

Howard Carter wrote the 2nd verse.
(Chairman of A/G . UK 1940)

Breathe oh breathe Thy breath upon us
Fan a mighty flame
'Till the fetters that have bound us
Break, in Jesus' name.
Burn in every heart the message
We must share with men
Send us Lord, a great revival
Breathe on us again.

Like a rushing wind from Heaven
Like as oil and dew
Like a river in the desert
Making all things new
Like the rain upon the meadow,
Like as tongues of fire.
Send us, Lord, the holy Spirit,
Young and old inspire.

Sinners weeping at the altar
Saints renewed with power
All backsliders coming Home, Lord
'Tis the midnight hour
Wayward sons and wayward daughters
End their useless search,
Finding joy and peace they longed for
In the old home Church.

SHOW ME

1st verse by Howard Carter

Show me Thy Passion, oh show it to me
The thorns and the scourging, the nails and the tree.
Thy sacred Blood flowing, Thy spear-wounded side
Oh show me Thy Passion, my Lord crucified.

Show me Thy Power oh show it to me
The power that o'er Death has triumphed gloriously..
Extended to all who by faith will receive
Oh show me Thy power, my Lord, I believe!

Show me Thy Purpose, oh show it to me
What Thou hast predestined from Eternity.
Unsearchable wisdom and knowledge and grace!
Oh show me Thy purpose, thy plan and my place.

Show me Thy Purchase, oh show her to me
The Church of the first-born The Lamb's wife-to-be.
The treasure You gave all you had to acquire,
Oh show me Thy purchase in bridal attire!

ROUSED BY THE BUGLE

War horses one day were put out to graze,
Left there in peace to enjoy their last days
Quietly, restfully, being at ease
Free from commands now,
   they do as they please

One day there came hunters with foxes and hounds
The Bugle was blasting its "Tally-Ho" sounds
And all those old horses, though long since retired
Were roused by the call all revived and inspired

They stood to their feet with their heads in the air
Ready for action to go anywhere!
The call of the bugle old memories had wakened
They lined up for warfare, but they were mistaken!

But many-a-saint who has thought his work finished,
Resting at ease, with his strength all diminished,
Hearing a "sound in the mulberry trees"
Will be stirred by the Spirit, and rise from his knees
Finding his strength is renewed as his youth
Gladly he'll go forth proclaiming the Truth.
Out in the front line, the foe to combat,
He won't be mistaken; he'll know "This is That——"
(Joel 2)

Printed in Evangel 1975
by Gospel publishing House.

11

MISSION

The Church has left the building, the Service has begun!
We're out here preaching Jesus and Satan's on the run!
Too long we've sat in chapel singing anthems in the choir
And seldom given a thought for those who're sinking in the mire.

The Highways and the Byways are strewn with broken lives,
They thought that they were flying high until they took a dive
And crashed amid the wreckage on a pathway of despair
Then someone went and told them of a loving God who cares

Rise up, oh Church of Jesus Christ and cast away your fears
Go; seek the lost before your youth is lost in fleeting years
Invade the world of darkness, and turn the night to day
Reveal the One who is the Light, the Truth the Life the Way.

DEUTERONOMY 32:10-13

He found him in a desert place,
A waste and howling land
Instructed him in ways of grace
And led him by the hand
He kept him and preserved him as the apple of His eye
Then stirred the nest,
Disturbed his rest
And taught him how to fly!

He gave him food in famine,
He gave him drink in dearth
He said "You'll ride upon the highest places of the earth"
And all his many enemies before him false would prove,
He said that He would love him with an everlasting love.

TWELVE BASKETSFUL

"Gather up the fragments that remain" the Master said.
"Let none of it be wasted, this precious fish and bread"
Too good to leave for flying fowl, this wonderful provision
It is for those who follow Him,
That was the Lord's decision

Twelve basketsful were gathered
One to each disciple given?
I cannot tell, but this is plain
There is much more, much more to gain
Than one meal's satisfaction.

Hunger to the church returned
And for a fragment Luther yearned
"This truth," he said "I will restore"
So nailed his Thesis to the door

The Church has now digested well
That fragment some thought came from hell
Time sorts things out and Truth remains
Then the whole cycle starts again!

Another "fragment seeker' captured
The Truth about the Church's rapture
"Second Comers" they were called"
Then came Healing preachers bold.

Pentecostal Gifts restored
Fragments from His bounteous store

And I believe there are some more
Precious fragments to explore
With hope and joy and gratitude

We'll find that Mercy's magnitude
Saves ALL of Adam's race!

BLACK MOUNTAIN CHOIR OF WALES

From rugged hills and verdant glen, this dedicated choir
Brings melody and harmony that meet the heart's desire.
When tenor voices soar above, with all their manly might,
We feel the strength of mountain climbs, the awe of
Snowdon's height.
Their Songs reflect the beauty of the land from which they come,
With softness, sensibility and sound second to none.

The baritones and bass go deep with rhythm and with rhymes,
They take us to the depths beneath, deep navigation mines.

*We hear the tender pathos of the mother's who have lost
Their children 'neath the fallen slag, (We'll never know the cost!)

A harpist and a Soloist named Leinor Daniel
With graceful style and winning smile can play the harp so well.
Her voice rings out with clarity, her diction is superb.
When singing Welsh or English, we can understand each word.
SING ON Black Mountain Choir of Wales
And keep our Flag unfurled.
You have a Ministry in Song

Go out and bless the world!

*

*Aberfan Disaster 1966. A mountain of Slag slid down,
burying a school full of children and teachers.*

WAITING FOR ISAIAH 35
TO BE FULFILLED

Don't tell me "It's natural, God made them that way"
When ravenous beasts hunt down innocent prey
And sink their big teeth in the jugular vein
'Till blood gushes out and they cry out in pain

.

Our God did not make them to kill and destroy
That's a lie from the Devil, a deceptive ploy
To make people think that the Lord doesn't care
When really, the blame lies on man's shoulders square.

.

It's too bad that Adam ate forbidden fruit
And forfeited power over Nature to boot
In crass disobedience he thwarted God's plan
For Earth to be tempered and controlled by man.

But Jesus, His power over Nature displays
By calming the winds and rebuking the waves.
In virtue of His perfect manhood He reigns
And power and dominion o'er all things reclaims.

Not taking advantage of His Deity
He shows us the way human nature should be.
And when He returns with His saints here to reign
He'll bring restoration of all things again.

KNITTED JACKETS

Knitted jackets made with care
Come with love and with a prayer
That you will realize some day
That God took strands of DNA
And knitted them within the womb,
A child was born, and that was you!

What workmanship the Lord has wrought
With infinite potential fraught
What you will be is your free choice
So listen for the "still small Voice"

* * * *

The Revised Standard Version reads-

"—Thou didst knit me together in my mother's womb—"
Psalm 139:13

THE AUCTION

They pay a million dollars a picture to obtain
A painting of some flowers in a two-by-four foot frame.
They hang it an the wall, and then protect with utmost care
A painting that a starving Artist made!

That's nothing new
That's what men do!
They worship the creation
Forgetting the Creator who deserves remuneration!

MEDITATION

My inner self requires that I should come apart
From earth's cacophony of noise
And find within the silent depths, a poise,
An attitude of receptivity
Openness for creativity.

I view the midnight canopy above the world,
And marvel at the jewels that were hurled,
Spinning and rotating, each within its sphere
And wonder if they're like the earth down here!

Are they inhabited with people like our human kind?
('Though not of Adam's race) And did the Serpent find
Another place to cause some serious panic
Contaminating yet another Planet?

I cannot tell, but this I know
That if Sin entered, the whole Universe defiling,
Christ, Life's Author, has by Death defying,
Made a value, that, with all our trying

Cannot be computed here in earthly terms.
Which goes to prove, and thus affirms-
No human wisdom touched that height!
It leaps across all boundaries
T'ward the Infinite.

OLD AGE

Old age is surely coming with all its aches and pains
Is that what we anticipate, bent backs and walking canes?
Nursing Homes with purred food and coffee stale and cold?
They say "It doesn't come alone" this state of getting old.

They say "It's second childhood," and in some ways,
I guess they're right,
But I'm not getting old—oh no!. —well, not without a fight!
I'll keep my fingers busy with knitting pins and yarn
The pots and pans I'll use each day while cooking up a storm!

Sometimes I make those 'granny squares' and use a
crochet hook.
I'll keep my mind well occupied with Bible and with books.
There's family and Christian friends, a gift of God indeed,
I know they'll be here helping me if ever I'm in need.

PSALM 17:15

"When I awake in His likeness, I shall be satisfied"

There's something that I want to say.
I don't know what it is!
I wish I did, I'd say it then, and get it over with!
I wonder what this feeling is that's bursting at the seams.
The concept of a symphony, a painting or vain dreams?

No, it is real, this yearning and this nagging at my soul,
It causes strong and forward thrusts toward an
unknown goal,
And so poetic lyrics flow unbidden from my pen.
I guess one day I shall express just what it is, and then,
I'll close my eyes,
Be satisfied,
And open them in Heaven.

*Written for the 75ᵗʰ Anniversary of the North Central Bible
Institute that later became College, then University.*

NCU

Fifteen and threescore years have passed, the plan of God unfolding,
A thousand lives each year go through the processes of molding
Then "Vessels unto Honour" formed by loving nail-scarred Hands
Are used in God's great Kingdom here at home and foreign lands,

To teach God's Word with power is the vision that they had,
It started in the Chapel of the Lake Street "Gospel Tab"
Frank Linquist and his wife, Irene, with those in teaching, skilled
Met there each day and found indeed, their vision was fulfilled,

The students kept on coming, until enrollment grew,
Crowding out the Chapel by filling every pew,
And then the Lord provided, in His providential care,
A Hospital that was for sale, with lots of room in there.

But I'll not dwell on buildings, and the way the Lord provided,
I'm more concerned with what they learned-
The truth " rightly divided,"
All through the years 'mid toil and tears, financial burdens too,
Our faith has never faltered, and we proved that God
'came through'

PEARLS FROM PAIN

Sand is fun to play in, but one little grain
Can cause any oyster incredible pain,
And over the irritant he will secrete
A fluid called Nacre, to bring him relief.

But after a while the old pain will return.
And to the poor oyster will feel like a burn,
The greater the pain, the greater the gain
In the size of the pearl that will form.

The Nacre envelops the jewel that develops
In travail, a rare pearl is born.
The lesson is clear, to all that will hear,
"His grace is sufficient for thee"

And so let us pray that when ills come our way,
We shall yield to the One who's the Giver
Of grace full and free
To you and to me
And allow Him the anguish to cover.
Believe in our character, He will create
Something of beauty forever!

Proverbs 7.25-27

THE SPIDER

It's simply amazing, that one sticky thread
Can be spun by a Spider to create her web
Octagonal ladders lead to her domain,
She waits there with hunger, her victim to claim.

Along comes a Suitor with amorous intent.
She stays on her Throne as she savors the scent
That wafts to her olfactory nerves on the breeze,
"I'll get him", she vows. "I'll bring him to his knees!"

Oh innocent victim, if only you knew
That others have been through this ordeal too
And ended a dastardly death to endure,
As the Queen of the Web made her banquet secure.

This one's no exception, and after they mate,
This carnivorous female lets him meet his fate!
The web looked attractive, all dappled with dew,
A thing of great beauty and delicate too.

Oh learn from the Spider
The truth I will tell — —

So often the Pathway to Fun leads to Hell..

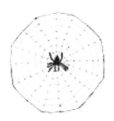

He sees the fox run to his rest
The nightingale fly to her nest, and muses,
'Earth must be my bed,
I have nowhere to lay my Head'
Was 'ere a lonelier Man than He? rejected by His family
And by Society?

Now up the mountain path He goes
The crowds disperse, and Jesus knows
They'll all be gone, He'll be alone,
For none invite Him to their home.

He fed them, taught them healed and blessed
Now they have all gone home to rest

Soon He climbs another hill, His sacrificial Blood to spill
And from 'defeat' at Calvary
Wrests triumphs of His Victory.
Up from the grave the Saviour rose,
Conquering death and all our foes

The Watchman waits at Heaven's Gates
That wondrous sight to see
As through the clouds, the Hero comes
In wounded Victory.
He shows His Hands, his Feet, His Side,
Declares "For Adam's race I died"

All Heaven's standing there in awe
The Watchman cries "Lift up the door"
The King of Glory shall come in.
The Father welcomes Him back Home,
And says "Well done, well done My Son"

Let Heaven's gates stay open wide,
The Son of God once crucified has full atonement made.
Oh wondrous grace, Oh Love Divine,
Now, sons of Adam. Heaven's thine!

Poem by David B. Owen for an Anniversary

❧❦❧❦❧❦❧❦

I've walked beside you through the winding years,
Through sunny laughter and through misty tears,
God's wondrous grace and clasp upon our hands
Has blessed our journey o'er life's shifting sands

I've walked beside you since our Wedding day
'Though golden locks are streaked with silver gray,
The love within my heart no fading knows
But with each passing year still deeper grows.

I'll walk beside you through all time to come
'Till we shall reach our heavenly Home sweet home,
And then upon that glorious shining strand,
I'll walk beside you, dearest, hand in hand!

❧❦❧❦❧❦❧❦

*I think he wrote this poem I found with alterations,
like a first draft!*

Your mercy heard my earliest prayer
Your grace and tender loving care
Sustained my youthful days.

Your goodness watched my ripening youth
And taught my heart to love Thy Truth,
And filled my life with praise,

Now in old age, your holy Name
Still burns within me like a flame
And bows my feeble knee.
My heart still knows how to rejoice,
My quivering voice has yet a Song for Thee…

A WEDDING PRAYER

*By David B. Owen On the occasion
of his Wedding to Heather Mavis Collins
Feb. 22 1947*

*Oh Lord, our prayer we raise to Thee, that Thou wilt bless always
The sweet and sacred unity of hearts made one, this day
Let many-splendored flowers of love life's trellis beautify
Do Thou watch o'er them from above
with gracious guiding eye*

*Not Eden's primal state we ask, where pleasure knew no pain,
Nor yet perennially to bask in sunshine with no rain,
No rose without a thorn doth bloom, No gain without a loss,
No glow of day without night's gloom,
No crown without a cross.*

*But if thy grace to those be given who now in love unite,
Their days on earth shall be as heaven, the heaviest cross be light,
The thorniest rose shall sweetness shed to stem the bitter tear
And in the darkest cloud of dread,
The rainbow will appear.*

*Then let Heaven's benedictive
smile on them oh Lord alight,
And grant that every winding mile
shall yield some new delight
Let love's harmonious happiness
ennoble all their days
And every passing hour express
Thy glory and thy praise.*

Feb 22, 1947:

Rev. David B. Owen marries Heather M Collins of Bromley Kent, UK

YOUTH MARCH

By David B. Owen
1944

Rise, rise ye blithesome youth
Enlist in our Crusade for Truth,
Oh enter now the field.
Take. take for glittering sword, your Good Excalibur, God's Word,
And faith, your royal Shield.

Christ our captain, Christ our life,
And Christ our strength in battle strife,
We onward march with conquering might
Nor cease contending for the right
Beneath the uplifted cross we fight
'Till every foe shall yield.

Raise, raise our songs on high
Resolved, for Christ to live or die,
We battle joyfully.
Vain, vain the foe doth press, the ranks of Christ know no distress
Nor ought shall make us flee.

Jesus' blood we magnify,
His empty tomb our battle cry
Our fortress strong His mighty Name
Our 'blazoned sign His Cross of shame,
Baptized with Pentecostal Flame
We march to victory!

Evil's day shall end in tears
And leave youth mangled 'neath the years,
But they who youth for Jesus spend
Shall youth possess that knows no end
For unto these it shall extend
Through heaven's eternal day!

On my 21ˢᵗ Birthday David gave me a locket and said——

*"Oh may this locket made of gold,
their likenesses enshrine
Whose hearts each other's image hold,
bound close in love's entwine.
Resistless, drawn by love's allure, so
tender sweet and strong,
It shall tenaciously endure as life's
years roll along."*

1946 David sent this little note to me
Once more 'mid solitudes of night
On wings of love my thoughts take flight
to my own darling, Heather.
No mocking miles can wholly part true love
and love's true counter-part.
In heart, we're still together.

2006
Now that he is with the Lord I think that he would write…
"And now from Heaven's shining light
On angel Wings, my thoughts take flight
To my own widow, Heather,
Not even death can wholly part true love and love's true
counter-part,
Somehow we're still together!"

THE LOON

Away from the city and man-
made distractions
I sought God's handiwork,
nature's attractions
The boundary waters beckoned me with unmistaken lure,
And there in sweet tranquility,
I breathed fresh air, so pure!
The quiet waters lapped around the boat as I was fishing
And then I thought I heard an Angel voice
that whispered "Listen"
I hearkened with intensity and in the distance heard.
That haunting awe-inspiring cry-
The Minnesota bird!

THE PEACOCK

In the Castle grounds at Cardiff South Wales.

The Peacock struts with steady pace around
the well-groomed lawn
And shows his multi-coloured tail, as tourists all look on,
What beauty in those feathers that fan out in
bold display!
The humble little hen looks on, she's simply
pale and gray,
"Just lay the eggs and hatch the chicks" that's
what she has to do,
While he can flaunt to other hens, and
mesmerize them too!

Thoughts at the Library

NO OTHER WAY.

If we could run our fingers
Up and down the spine
Of paper, leather or whatever,
And in no time find
The poetry, philosophy and history of our times
Imparted quite miraculously into our open minds,
Would we appreciate the skill that went into their craft?
The work of thoughts put into words, revising draft on draft?
Would we enjoy the language and the nuance of each sound?
Oh no! There is no detour round the mountain of hard work,
We cannot by-pass studying
And think that we can shirk
The path that others trod to get to where they are today.
Let's put our "specks" on
Read those books,
There is no other way!

SALISBURY CATHEDRAL

A lofty spire so stately stands in Salisbury's verdant plains
It is the highest one in England and in other lands.
Towering o'er the roof-tops and the tallest of the trees,
It's there as a reminder to everyone who sees
That.like the spire, portraying hands together pointing high
We ought to offer prayer and know He hears our faintest cry;

For centuries the saints have come
to worship and beseech
The Lord, Whose image art
portrays where Bishops
stand to preach.
Those song-soaked walls now
silent hold many-a-secret prayer
As worshippers poured out their
hearts and cast on God their care.
If only, in this modern day of
electronic skill
We could back-up two hundred
years, recapturing the thrill
Of antiphonal singing sound
Medieval glass in lead resound,
And hear the organ swell!

BLACK DIAMONDS

Buried down deep for a few million years,

Growing real ancient with all of my peers

Heat and great pressure is all that we knew.

'Till one day a miner decided to hew.

We were rudely dislodged from our home in the seam,

Thrown in a tub, taken up to the screen,

Sorted and sifted to big chunks and small...

Slag was discarded- our tub's on a roll.

They call us" Black Diamonds:"

We're anthracite coal!

The last time that we were exposed to the sun

Is when we were oak trees and we were all young,

How well we remember our days 'in the leaf'

And then the wind blew, and we all came to grief!

Down in the dirt we were trampled and bruised

Knowing not, some day for fuel we'd be used.

We keep the fires burning in many a home,

And industry's wheels turning round with a drone.

Now, what would life be if it were not for coal?

We'd better thank God for that's good for the soul.

NATURE IN MINNESOTA

She ransacks her wardrobe of colours so gay,

To deck all the trees on that first Autumn day

Too short is the month of October each year

When leaves are resplendent with colour and cheer.

So soon they will fade and be blown in the wind

Trees will be bare and will lose everything,

Do not despair, for this is not the end,

They die with sure hope of new life in the Spring

*   *   *

God's "Second Man" was wounded for me

Perfect humanity nailed to a tree

"Author of Life" yet the Lamb that was slain

"The Great Resurrection". was buried in vain.

MARRIAGE

The honeymoon's over,
You married a saint!
Well, that's what you thought 'till you found that he ain't!
Please pardon the grammar, but isn't it true,
Nobody's perfect, not me and not you?

That "virtuous woman" 'Song of Solomon' gives
As the perfect example of how we should live!
I've never met anyone yet who aspires
To be "Venus perfectos" whom all men desire.

She's up before dawn making cinnamon rolls
Then out buying real estate
Setting new goals,
She's quite unbelievable, you must concur
That the famed Martha Stewart has nothing on her!

This wonderful girl's skilled with needle and thread,
She clothes all her family in flannel that's red!
Well, that wouldn't do in this day and age,
But it's clear. You determine the way kids behave.

You choose what they wear, for there is right and wrong.
Be modest; don't buy a bikini or thong!

And now guys, it's your turn to hear some "home truth"
Don't try to recapture the days of your youth
With trendy coiffures and designer-made suits,
Or hair styled like hippies with tall cowboy boots.

You come home from work and you kick off your shoes
Before you say "Hi" you are taking a snooze.
Then dinnertime comes "oh it's turkey and dressing!
That's what we had yesterday!"
-"just ask the blessing!
Don't grumble at left-overs, now listen Honey,
It's the end of the month and I've spent all the money!"

Does that sound familiar? Well boys, join the club!
Be thankful she knows how to fix up the grub,
She knows how to stretch it and make the ends meet
And dresses the kids from their heads to their feet.

She keeps the house clean and she washes the clothes
Her work's never-ending, that, everyone knows!
God said "he who finds a wife finds a good thing"
So value the meaning of your wedding ring!

Divine invasion of humanity!
The footprints of the God-man on our Earth.!
I see them with the eye of faith, and exclaim
"Lord come again.
And end the pain,
The famine and the dearth."

The footprints of Earthman upon the moon
Bespeak the end of all things coming soon,
For as we seek to conquer outer space,
Invading other worlds with frantic pace
'Gainst time, whose sand so quickly fills the glass,
One has to ask
What is the driving force?
All this shall pass!

We're made for better things than this old Earth,
We're made for higher things of priceless worth
Created for a destiny
Created for Eternity.
His wisdom and His grace to show
To worlds as yet unborn.

And in the ages yet to be
If one should say
"Lord let me see Thy grace and wisdom manifest."
He'll turn to us, His Church, His Bride
And say with pride,
"Here's wisdom and here's grace
Personified."

When you see the fig tree blossom, and all the trees
When you see the fig tree blossom, putting forth its leaves,
Then you'll know the hour is drawing near, When the heavenly Bridegroom shall appear.
When you see the fig tree blossom,
Fall on your knees

Bible Scholars agree that the fig tree is a type of Israel.
It blossomed in 1948!

EZEKIEL 37:9

Everything shall live where the River flows!

The desert shall blossom as the rose

Barren soul rejoice, for you shall bear

Fruit that shall abound everywhere.

ISRAEL

Watching alone o'er Jerusalem, it was Jesus of Nazareth
Weeping in sorrow for love of them
Who so soon would acclaim His Death.
Then He turned from His vigil with saddened face,
But the words that He spoke still resound,
"Oh how oft I'd have gathered you unto me!"
They were lost, and refused to be found!

Blindness has happened to Israel,
Who for centuries awaited that day,
Messiah had come.
And they knew Him not,
They rejected and cast Him away…
But the time soon will come when with open eyes
They will look on the Lamb glorified,
And repent of their sin, and acknowledge Him
As Messiah, and with Him abide.

THE TRANSFIGURATION

The Disciples on the height of the mountain saw the light

And the splendor of our transfigured Lord,

Peter said "Now let us stay

And build three alters here today,

It's so good to get away

From it all!"

But I'm glad he changed his plan.

Thought he'd lend a helping hand,

For a lunatic was waiting down the hill…

Blessed be the Son of God

Who the path of suffering trod.

He didn't get away

From it all!

But he promised He would stay

With His people, 'till that day

When He'd reconcile the whole world to God!

JESUS BLESSED JESUS

There is a Name, a Saving name
Jesus blessed Jesus,
On Angel lips from Heaven it came,
Jesus blessed Jesus.
He came to lift our fallen race,
He took the guilty sinner's place,
That all may taste his pardoning grace,
Jesus blessed Jesus.

There is a name, a Healing Name,
Jesus, blessed Jesus,
Its ancient power is still the same,
Jesus, blessed Jesus,
The maimed, the deaf, the dumb, the blind,
The sick in body and in mind,
Its healthful virtue still may find
Jesus. Blessed Jesus.

There is a Name, Hope-kindling Name,
Jesus blessed Jesus,
Through darkening years, shines on, the flame
Jesus. Blessed Jesus,
Unfailing stands His promise plain,
Nor cherish we this hope in vain,
In splendor soon He'll come again,
Jesus blessed Jesus.

There is a Name, a Sovereign Name,
Jesus, blessed Jesus,
The whole creation shall acclaim
Jesus blessed Jesus.
All Heaven and Hell and Earth and Sea
Before that Name shall bow the knee,
Twill ring through all eternity,
Jesus blessed Jesus.

I CHRONICLES 13

Pick up the trumpet and sound an alarm.

Alert God's people to imminent harm,

The Scripture has warned us, the world to forsake,

Its methods and practices

Christians should hate.

God told us the way we should carry the Ark,

It isn't the worldly way, on a new cart,

Trinkets and idols we'll throw to the wind

Lest God should smite us because we have sinned.

Pray for Revival the old fashioned way

God surely will answer before that great Day.

Let's meet the conditions, the price we must pay,

The Ark must be carried, and Christians must pray.

A Christ-centered message and people that sing

Songs that exalt the Lord Jesus as King,

Rejecting the subjective chorus and Hymn

Lift Jesus high and the world He will win...

FAITH

I face reality
My hand in His.
Be gone my fantasies
I want to live
Not like the desert bird
Fearing the foe,
Hiding his head in sand
Thinking 'twill go!

I face reality
My head held high
Sorrow or ecstasy, the Lord is nigh
..And so whatever comes my way
I'll not forget
That "He who hath and doth deliver
Will deliver yet"

1ˢᵗ verse by Howard Carter 1944

THE POTTER

O Potter of the living clay,
Thy perfect work is marred
The vessel fair is spoiled by sin,
Created glory scarred.
Upon the wheel of Providence
Mould me by grace Divine,
A vessel unto honour make
With loveliness like Thine

O Potter of the living clay
What skilful work is Thine,
That erstwhile ruined man, some day
May in Thine image shine!
And in those heavenly places will
Ethereal Beings tell
The wonder of the Potter's skill
Who has done all things well.
He made it again, even though it had been marred
He made it again, without reference to
its scars,
The Potter saw me in His plan
Shaped me in His nail-scarred Hand
He'll restore, evermore, fallen man.

Show me the Shikinah

Drench me with a shower,

Clothe me with the mantle

Let me use the power,

Lord God of Elijah

Where art Thou?

Come and work a miracle now Lord, now

Springs of living water bubbling through the clay,

Cleansing, purifying us

From day to day.

Flow thou mighty river,

Free us from all dearth

Life and health reviving

Saturate the earth.

I wrote this in 1975. It goes to the tune of"
Love's Old Sweet Song"

Long have I walked the straight and narrow way
Long have I known His love from day to day
His peace and joy, my portion sure have been,
Yet something deeper in Him I have seen,
Lord. There's a yearning in the "inner man"
Grant revelation of thy perfect plan

Chorus
O that I might know Him,
This is my desire,
Resurrection power,
Pentecostal fire!
Fellowship in suffering,
In my body bear marks of His affliction
His crown to wear
And Calvary's triumph share.

All consecrations culminated here,
All self-assertion now must disappear
All of ambitions proud and ugly head
Here must be buried and be reckoned dead
Risen Redeemer bring forth in its place
All that was purchased for me by thy grace.

THE CROSS

Some day I'll understand the Saviour's death upon the tree
Some day I'll scale the heights and plumb
the depths of mystery,
Great purposes, beyond the comprehension of the mind
Man's spirit, understanding from the Lord Almighty finds.
It seems to me like sacrilege to question and to probe,
To 'dare stretch out the hand' to touch the
thorns and purple robe,
I do not ask the wounded side and nail prints to see,
"My Lord, My God" I humbly cry
And bow and worship Thee.

"There is a spirit in man, and by it he getteth
understanding from the Almighty"
Job 32: 8

ROMANS 8:28

Everything's included in the "all things
That work together for good"
Everything's included in the "all things"
That's settled and understood!
Jesus hasn't said that our free will, He'd override,
We will make mistakes, but know the Saviour's on our side,
And when we get together when ends life's little day
We'll se that somehow, in His wisdom, He has had his way!
The Purposes of God are fixed, and all will be fulfilled
The Plan of God is flexible, because of our free will,
But He will work things out for good,
Unfolding through the years,
So dance upon the mountain tops
Or tread the vale of tears.
One day we'll see the cosmic view of all that's taken place,
And marvel at His wisdom,
And praise him for his grace…

JACOB

He blessed him there
The place where he had wrestled
Until the day dawned in the eastern sky.
He blessed him there, and teaches me this lesson-
If I would live, then this old self must die,

He blessed him there,
The place of full submission
To what the Lord of Heaven would have him be.
He blessed him there, destroying vain ambition.
Jacob subdued, now Israel we see!

O Thou who art the God of Jacob ever,
Who changes not, 'though all things else may fail.
Give me the touch, all sinful ties to sever,
Grant me the princely Power that must prevail.

THE GOLDEN YEARS

"Where is the gold in the "golden years?"
Somebody asked, through a mist of tears,
It's simply a matter of value sense!
To some its dollars or pounds and pence,
To others, it's what they have put in store
Of memories precious from days of yore,

So while you're young and care-free and fine,
Create occasions that you will, in time
Re-live and enjoy all over again,
Then if you're lonely, and may be in pain.
Be thankful that you can remember the past
And recall so much that has caused you to laugh

Things that the children have said or have done,
The trophies and accolades some of them won,
Recapture the pride and the joy that you felt
When life was such fun and a "good hand was dealt"
You were happy back then, so be happy today
There's much to thank God for, so praise Him and pray!

1997: 50ᵗʰ Wedding Anniversary

HYMN

In Him dwelleth all the fullness of our God,
Yet a Servant's form He took, and earth He trod.
Man he understands because He knows our frame
And remembers that from Eden's dust we came.
He's the Breath that breathed upon this earthly clay,
And makes me live for aye!

He can full deliverance to the captive bring,
He can heal the broken heart and make it sing,
He's the Key Divine that fits the human lock,
He'd the gentle Shepherd; we're the erring flock,
He's the only Answer to the world's great need,
He is the Christ, indeed!

He will never break the reed that has been bruised,
He will yet restore the life that sin abused,
Staying wrath and judgment, grace and mercy flow,
Thus shall all men Christ the Lord as Saviour know,
Every knee shall bow and tongue confess Him Lord
'Tis written in His Word.

RISE UP WITH WINGS
LIKE THE EAGLE

When tempest storms are raging,

That's when the Eagles fly.

They soar above the altitude where frightened seagulls cry!

Let's spread our wings of faith and rise

Upon the upward breeze

And see the lovely rainbow, all three sixty degrees!

Below, we only catch a glimpse of all God has in store,

But in our flight, and on the height

Encounter so much more!

WINTER STORM

'Twas there for days!, How blind was I to miss a sight so rare
I'd been driving down the Highway with a blind hypnotic stare
And had not even seen the beauty there against the blue
'Till now, when trees are shimmering with a coat of silver hue.
I see a million rainbows all reflecting Winter's Sun
And myriads of snow flakes that fell softly by the ton!
And I exclaim," Lord, thank you for prismatic beauty rare
Help me to be observant, for your beauty's everywhere!

Bless us, bless us.
Come and refresh us
Open thy bountiful hand
Like the dew falling
New every morning
Silently covering the land,
Purify, justify, sanctify, glorify.
So let Thy doctrines distill
Bless us. Bless us,
Come and refresh us,
Drench every valley and hill, drench every valley and hill!.

Nostalgia

Give back our songs that were doctrinally sound,
With music unmatched and with truth that's profound,
We, who were raised on those beautiful hymns,
Are starving for meaning, not ditties and whims!

We've exercised grace 'till we're sick and we're tired
Of untrained "musicians" who ought to be fired!
Oh why did we ever leave our mother Church
For freedom, that simply left us in the lurch?

Now where is the writer, the painter, the bard?
Or where is the sculptor? Oh let us well guard
The artistry men long since gone, have bequeathed,
Their work still lives on, and we know it's God-breathed!

SHORT CUT?

There's no short cut to godliness,
There's no short cut to Gain,
Sometimes the way to holiness will take the path
of pain,
There's effort and there's sacrifice in anything
worthwhile,
So by God's grace
Just run the race
And go the extra mile!

JESUS

He left Eternity, entered Time,
Embraced limitations of human-kind,
Lived as a man with God's Spirit anointed,
To be "Heir of all things", as God had appointed.

"We see, not yet all things put under His feet"
But He will return with His saints, and will meet
The enemy here, and the war He will win,
(He's already conquered original sin)

And then Armageddon, that battle at last
When into bondage the Devil is cast.
Peace over all things!
Forever He'll reign.
Life will be Eden all over again.

OBSERVATION

Emotion and volition,

Components of decision!

If choice is made with one and not the other

Results will be unstable,

And you will be unable

To keep the promise and pursue the path.

I CORINTHIANS 13

Here is Paul's analysis with some component parts
That go towards comprising what surpasses all the arts.
There's Something here too big for human minds to
comprehend,
For God Himself bears that great name,
He's LOVE beyond our ken.

Accept the God of love and you will definitely find
That you can be most patient, suffering long and still be kind,
Love shelters and protects, does not expose another's fault
But helps him and protects him from falling in sin's vault.

Love never celebrates misfortune of a precious soul,
Nor spreads around a rumor that on someone took its toll
Love does not boast about the many things it has achieved,
Nor ask for its own way and cause another heart to grieve.

Our God is LOVE, and LOVE is God,
Keep Him in life, the center
Then some glad day. You'll hear Him say
"Well done! Here's Heaven, Enter!"

CHANGING TIMES

The songs we sing, the clothes we wear,
The way we talk and do our hair
Reflect the culture of our day,
And it has always been that way.

In other times they were precise,
In speech, dress hair-do's and the like
Well-mannered kids and tidy home
That's how our character was known.

It's different now, a new age dawns,
The older generation mourns
To see the "standards" go so fast,
But nothing will for ever last!

Let's blow our noses, dry our tears
And live another twenty years,
We read "that there remaineth yet
Much land to conquer", so let's get
With this new generation and forget
Those "good old days!"

SPIRITUAL LESSON

1 Chronicles 15:11and Samuel 5:16 & 23

After the revival, the king went on his way,
With good intent to bless his wife and say
"The Ark of God is here at last
No longer need we pray and fast.
But now rejoice and dance before the Lord"

Now Michael, David's wife was vain,
She gave that look of proud disdain
And with sarcastic tone of voice
Said," Glorious was your Kingly choice
To dance before them on the road,
And even drop your Royal robe,
You're just like common men!"

Oh Michael, if you only knew
That blessing was for them and you,'
Despise it if you will and think it wild,
But you will pay the price and you will live your life
In barrenness
For you shall have no child!

ILLUMINATION

Give me a light that does not blind,
But just enlightens me.
Help me the tangled strands unwind
To set the treasure free,
I'm prone to get distracted with the
dogmas and the form
Losing the Message, and alas! Find that the truth's been shorn
Of absolutes, of black and white,
And in their place is given
An area of questioning regarding Hell and Heaven.

We're living in a day and age of such uncertainty
Where all time-honoured doctrines are under scrutiny
But truth will stand the test of time,
The Treasure will all gems outshine,
And Light will show the Way.

KEY NOTE

I hear the chords of dissonance, yet there's a basic sound,
One seems like sand beneath our feet, the other solid ground.
Life is a mixture of the two, that's what it's all about.

Unconsciously we recognize the turmoil in the earth
In chords that jar the ear, while bass holds on for all it's worth.
Like strains from Scottish bagpipes with their perpetual drone,
No matter what-they hold on fast to what is proved and known.

To stabilize the restlessness, the waywardness of youth
That tonic bass, with steady tone is there to welcome
wanderers Home
Where all may find the truth

The Great Creator never stops creating.

And so new songs are written every day

New inspiration given from the Master

His wisdom and His beauty to display

We're conduits of His infinite attributes

With poetry and music flowing through.

We manifest his love and grace and mercy

To those who never heard and never knew.

O what a privilege to take the Message

Whatever way our God sees fit to use

In preaching or in music or in painting

He has so many ways, hard hearts to move.

He will through us, His Bride, create some day

That perfect song that will through Heaven ring.

The language will surpass all prose and verse

And echo through the far-flung universe.

Now sin has gone, He lifts the curse,

Let all creation Sing!

WHAT'S WRONG WITH THE WORLD?

"What's wrong with the world?" that question you ask,

We search for a reason, formidable task!

Some say "natural causes," or "God is to blame!"

May be global-warming, the sun or the rain.

It's anything, everything, trump up a cause

Why man is not peaceful, but always in wars.

Blame politics, Presidents, Preachers. TV.

Blame anyone, everyone, but don't you blame me!

"What's wrong with the world? "many Pundits give reasons.

Biologists say there's a change in the Seasons,

It's pesticides, germicides plastics, tin foil,

It's nylon, synthetics, trans-fats and bad oil.

We can't eat the fish, it is mercury-laden

(All will be well now we've caught old Bin Laden)

Flouride in water. Pollutants in air,

So what can we do? We are doomed to despair!

"What's wrong with the world? "it is sure in a jam,

G.K. Chesterton answered quite simply I am' "

SOMETIMES

Sometimes we need to intercede
Sometimes we need to be quiet and read
Allowing the living Word to renew
The life and power that once we knew.

Sometimes we need to sing and shout
Sometimes we need to get up and get out
Leaving the joy of our comfort zone
Visiting those in the Nursing Home.

All day they sit with a frozen stare
Praying "Oh God, doesn't anyone care?"
True Christianity manifests grace
A word to the helpless brings smiles to their face

And when in Eternity with Christ we'll be
He may say: "Remember, you visited Me?

"Inasmuch as ye have done it unto one of the least of these
my brethren, ye have done it unto Me "

Matthew 25:40

PIANO LESSONS

Tip of your "pinkie" and side of your thumb
Curve all your fingers, now that's lesson one!
Lifting and striking the black and white keys,
Relax your shoulders, you'll play then with ease

Stretch between fingers that strengthen the muscles
That tie them together across all your knuckles.
Heel on the floor and your toes on the pedal
You're well on the way now to winning a medal (?)

It takes years of practice to be a musician
Your fingers must be in a real good condition.
Once that is mastered, we'll work on the wrists
Playing staccato with no sideway twists.

Now you'll play triads an octave apart
Using your forearm describing an arc
Some day, the big chords you'll play when you're older
The arm drop will then be not forearm, but shoulder

What fun it will be when you play for your friends,
With no need to fake it, no need to pretend
For now your read music and have a trained ear,
Good job! You have come a long way in a year!

SEEKING SATISFACTION

Deluded by illusion
Suffering from confusion
Famished by the food of fantasy,
Longing for Reality
Yearning for integrity,
Search in vain, and mocking mirage find!
Study the philosophy
Of Plato Freud or Socrates
And nothing there a broken heart can bind,
God calls for true repentance
A perfect turn-a-round,
The Cross of Calvary beckons me
That's where true Life is found!
The Truth is there personified,
In Christ, the Saviour crucified,
The search has ended here at last.
Forgiven is my wayward past.
And I am satisfied.

THE BUTTON BOX

There's a fancy box in the bureau drawer
Containing buttons and buckles galore
They all remind me of days of yore
Of old-time dresses and belts we wore.
There's a big black button off a winter coat
That daddy wore on a sailing boat.
A storm arose (oh I mind it well-)
He was "tacking' the sails, lost balance and fell.
He came back to the car all soaking wet,
Still in his coat and bowler hat.
Mother just gave him a look of disdain with "Idiot,
don't do that again"

There's a buckle made of mother of pearl that
Nanny wore when she was a girl
There are three marble buttons from the dress I wore at
Ken & Sal's wedding in '74.
All sizes and colours, a story could tell-wood,
pearl, ivory. marble and shell
It's not just the memories one can recall, but there
is a lesson that we should install
On a permanent disc with indelible grace,-no matter
what colour, what size or what shape,
We're all in the Button Box here for His glory.
The Craftsman has fashioned us,
End of story!

THE LOST SONG

That ancient Heavenly Song we are trying to recall
Was long –lost, maybe buried in Eden at the fall
Since then souls have been craving, with dedicated search
For some Celestial sound,
We try to hear it in the Church,

Sometimes a phrase or motif rare ignites our hopes again
And on we plod, asking for God to let us hear it plain.
We know it's there; the blue-print of that song is in the soul
We'll recognize it sing-a-long when we have reached the goal.
The "Vox Humana" now repaired, will sing the melody,
The "Universal Organ" will peel forth in harmony,
Then all Creation will resound, the stars again will sing
The sons of God will shout for joy,
For Jesus will be King.

78

WOMEN

Women have a special place in God's Redemptive plan
Right from the start, God said her seed would be the Second Man
Her offspring would, one day redeem a future fallen race,
And in the fullness of His time, He'd manifest His grace

All through the Scriptures, we find pictures,
Types of things to be,
The barren woman bears a promised child miraculously,
Sarah, Rachel, Hannah all point to a future girl,
A virgin who would bear the Christ,
The Saviour of the world.

Our status as the female sex, God rose to lofty heights
For God has given us a place of dignity and rights,
We can come boldly to the Throne
And touch the heart of Him
Who came through Rahab, Ruth and those
Who were of foreign kin.
As one great theologian wrote
"He came through all, to all, and for all people of the earth
Who're ruined by the Fall.
Thank God for women in the past that God placed in His plan,
For through the woman's seed, the Christ has rescued fallen man.

WOMEN IN MINISTRY

Whether you're a Teacher, a Pastor or his wife,
There's nothing quite like being in Ministerial life,
Sometimes you feel inadequate for all that is required
As day by day the same routine can make you less inspired,
But don't give up. It's worth it all, for you will hear folks say
"Oh, am I ever glad, dear friend that
you have passed my way"
We're not aware of influence or how we "come across'
The tender touch of sympathy when one's sustained a loss.
The simple prayer with someone who
is going through divorce-
Her heart is aching, breaking as she suffers deep remorse.
Let's keep our spirits sensitive to how His Spirit moves,
With open minds and steadfast faith, His promises to prove.
Oh Holy Spirit, come again
And fan these embers into flame,
Let love replace the apathy
And fill my heart with sympathy.
For I am nothing more than dust, without thee
Breath of Deity

THE LAMB

Revelation 5:5 & 6

John saw, in vision, a revelation of One who would
rule and would reign
And he looked for a Lion of the tribe of Judah and
beheld a Lamb that was slain.
Follow the Blood drops to Calvary's mountain
Follow the Blood drops again
Back to eternity, 'ere earth's foundation.
That's where, by faith. He was slain.

Jesus was led as a Lamb to the slaughter
Self-vindication subdued,
Willingly laying His life on the altar,
Dying for me and for you.
Oh for a quiet and peaceful spirit!
Gift of great value and worth!
Teach me submission, this blessing I covet.
The meek shall inherit the earth.

When all the wars and tumults are ended,
and Jesus reigns far above all,
His knowledge and glory the whole earth shall cover,
and at His feet all me shall fall,
All shall bow down to Him
All shall acknowledge Him
Lord of Lords, King of all Kings,
Death shall be swallowed in glorious victory,
Worthy the lamb we shall sing.

THE HOPE OF SPRING

Leaves are falling, falling fast,
Soon shall come the icy blast
Of Winter's cruel wind.

Snow, Earth's white protective cover
Guards the life of seeds sown under,
Springtime, when the sun comes out
Will coax the seedlings then to sprout.

Seedtime and Harvest still obtain,
And shall do while the Earth remains,
But when God's SON returns, He'll bring
The blessing of ETERNAL SPRING

11, 4 2006.

Communion

He didn't build a monument and say "Remember Me
Come to this place and gaze on it and humbly bow your knee"
If it were in Jerusalem, so few could 'ere afford
To make the trip, remember Him and thus obey the Lord..

But He has given us way- simplicity indeed!
And all can be His worshippers and His instructions heed.
"Just take a little bread and wine"
This method stands the test of time

It's durable, available, and accessible to all;
Remember Him, dwell on His death, the agony and gall.
Then praise Him, for He rose again,
And He is coming back to reign.

CALVARY MUST TRIUMPH

Calvary reversed the trend
That leads to eternal damnation
And on that road so broad, so wide,
He planted His cross of Salvation

With arms outstretched
From east to west,
And linking earth to Heaven,
He made a road—block to prevent
Humanity's inherent bent
And prays they'll be forgiven! (*Luke 23: 34*)

The devil will not ever say—
"Look God, there's more that came MY way
So Hell is full and You have failed_"
NO NEVER !
CALVARY HAS PREVAILED !

Matthew 7" 13 Jesus said these things BEFORE the Cross.

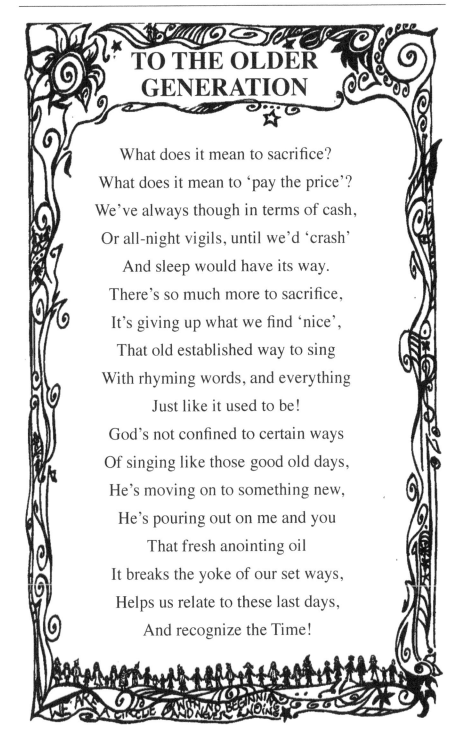

TO THE OLDER GENERATION

What does it mean to sacrifice?

What does it mean to 'pay the price'?

We've always though in terms of cash,

Or all-night vigils, until we'd 'crash'

And sleep would have its way.

There's so much more to sacrifice,

It's giving up what we find 'nice',

That old established way to sing

With rhyming words, and everything

Just like it used to be!

God's not confined to certain ways

Of singing like those good old days,

He's moving on to something new,

He's pouring out on me and you

That fresh anointing oil

It breaks the yoke of our set ways,

Helps us relate to these last days,

And recognize the Time!

INSPIRATION

Embryonic ideas, words evolving, jostling, communicating
As they float in the amniotic gray matter of the mind!
Finally, a sentence will emerge
And be thrust from the darkness of its cerebral womb.
Acceptance, rejection or mere indifference
Is the risk that's taken. hoping for receptivity,
Where its maturity will result
In the expression of a long-sought truth…
There is a Life-Force that ignites this whole procedure.
Conception takes more than one entity,
And so the human and Divine imaginations merge.

David & Heather Owen's sons & their wives:
From the left: Ken& Sally, Colin & Margie, Bill & Sherry & Dave & Dianna

87th Birthday

Time flies! And it takes so much with it,
All my youth and sparkle, but I still have my wit.
I've spent a fortune on those anti-age creams
That 'do wonders' —- in my dreams!
Waist line! What became of my waist line?
Everything has gone south
And I'm down in the mouth.
Chin almost on my chest—that used to be there!
But they won't fix it on Medicare.

Birthdays come and birthdays go
Another trip round the Sun.
This will add to my many years,
Twelve months- another one,
Years ? Yes I have lived Eighty seven
And I'm ready for Heaven,,
Just as soon as I'm called.
I've had a super life, and this I can say
"I AM SO GRATEFUL TO THE LORD!"

YOUTH RESTORED!

Old widower, Charlie, concerned with his looks
Decided to read a few ' health advice' books,
"Do those adverts" he wondered," contain any truth
.That Ginseng Tea drinkers would renew their youth ?"

He drank by the gallon that advertised potion
Hoping to set all his 'youth wheels;' in motion.!
One day he decided to marry again,
In spite of arthritis and many a pain.

His friends thought old Charlie had now lost his mind
When he went out searching, a widow to find.
He found her! a cute one who was the same age,
She too was near ninety and 'on the same page'

Now after the Wedding they went for a drink
Ginseng Tea of course !- now what else would you think?
Next morning ,his bride could not find him at home,
She thought that he must have gone out for a roam.

On the curb there she found him- lunch bag by his side.
He sobbed "There's the school bus,
I just missed my ride !"

A BAPTISM TO REMEMBER 1956
Milwaukee Gospel Tabernacle.

The Pastor in Milwaukee was a very heavy man,

He must have weighed 300 lbs and had a 9 inch span.

One Sunday he was absent for he had a holiday

So David took his place & preached the good old fashioned way,

Then thirty people sought the Lord & found his saving grace,

And all were robed in pristine white & slowly took their place

Upon the front row of the Church ,to be baptized that night.

"They" said it was the custom, Pastor's wet suit he must wear

To just wear ordinary clothes of this they would not hear.

So dutifully David donned the wet suit—extra large!

The Deacons were all happy then, for they were all in charge

The trouble was, that every time a candidate was dipped

About a gallon filled the gap where the wetsuit did not fit.

So when the thirty folks were all immersed and raised again,

It felt as though he'd been for ever in a flood of rain.

He was 'filled up' – so heavy was the water in the suit

He had to stand there in the pool & couldn't move a foot !

The deacons came and pulled him out & tipped him upside down.!!

Talk about a Circus Act ! The Preacher was the Clown!

A La Carte (The Golfer's lunch)

A club sand wedge

A slice of cake

A cup of green tee

A few chips.

Abbeys and Basilicas, Cathedrals of history
Resound with choral music and reveal to us the mystery
Of timeless deep emotion rooted in God's holy Word
That men of old expressed in song
Thus honoring the Lord.
The blend of human voices with their purity of tone
Cannot be matched by instruments, like cornet or trombone,
The organ has its place in Church, the brass and strings do too,
But there's no sound like vocal chords
From folks like me and you!
As long as we have found the art of singing 'from the core'
The tone and quality will leave us
Wanting nothing more.

Author UNKNOWN
England, my England

Goodbye to my England, so long my old friend.
Your days are all numbered, they'll come to an end.
You're Scottish or Irish, or Welsh? that's just fine,
But don't say you're English, that's way out of line.

The French & the Germans may call themselves such,
And so may Norwegians, the Swedes & the Dutch,
You can say you are Russian, or maybe a Dane
But don't say you're English, not ever again.

At Broadcasting House the word England's taboo
In Brussels it's scrapped & in Parliament too.
Our schools are affected, staff do as they're told
They must not teach kids about England of old.,

Writers like Shakespeare or Milton or Shaw,
The pupils don't learn about them anymore.
And how about Agincourt, Hastings or Mons
When England lost hosts of her very brave sons?

We're not European, now how could we be?
Europe is miles away, over the sea.
We're English from England so let's all be proud
Stand up and be counted, and shout it out loud.

Government, listen ! and Brussels. you too,
We're proud of our banner, the red white and blue.
Fly the flag of St George or the Union Jack,
And let the world know WE WANT OUR ENGLAND BACK!

Autumn Morn

I looked out of my window
On a lovely Autumn morn
And saw a million diamonds
Dancing on the new-mown lawn.
The scintillating colors,
All refractions of the light.
And as each blade moved in the breeze
It seemed, to my delight
As though some Heavenly Being
Had been working through the night
To bless the earth with rainbow hue
In every tiny drop of dew .
I'm thankful that each morning
He sends blessings that are new.
We serve a loving, faithful God,
His promises are true!.
Lamentations 3:22-23

AWESOME!!

What happened to good language?
Is it something from the past?
Kids go to greasy Food Stands
And get some food that's fast.
And what they say is
" Awesome, man !"
A sausage on a stick!!!
And then they get an ice cream cone
To hold, so they can lick!
One wonders if they've stopped to see
A sunset in the west,
Or stood upon a mountain Craig
And seen an eagle's nest
So many things are truly great
And "Awesome" would be right.
Don't let them prostitute our words
Without a verbal fight..

BAD NEWS__GOOD NEWS!

"And that's the way it is! "
As Walter Cronkite always said

After he read the daily news—
Then it was time for bed.

The lingering thoughts left me distraught;
The news was always bad.

Thank God ,He has not left us there
Stuck in "the way it IS"

He made the way it OUGHT to be
Through Jesus Christ on Calvary,

And for THAT news, I'm glad !

CONTRASTS

The pendulum swings, but seldom does one eighty,

In all of life there is variety,

Sunshine and shadow ,loss and gain,

Enjoy, endure, pleasure and pain,

There's birth and death

And much between,

Days of plenty, days of lean.

Think how boring life would be

Without an anniversary

A birthday or a holiday,

And family coming for a stay.

The contrast in Eternity

Is Heaven or Hell

Which shall it be ?

The Canary in the Window (a familiar sight in the mining districts of Wales)

He looks so cute there in his cage,
The kids all love him and they wave
As they go by to school.
He took a breath and met his death
And that's a serious sign
That there's a leak of gas down deep
In 'Navigation Mine'
A monument should be erected
To the birds who have detected
Gas, and saved mens' lives.
We honour men who lost their lives
And have their names in brass inscribed
On plaques and memorabilia,
But don't forget the childrens' pet
Who lost his life so men might get
Out of the Mine in time !

CULTURAL CURRENTS

CULTURAL CURRENTS WILL LEAD US ASTRAY.
BEWARE OF OPINIONS THAT MULTITUDES SAY
ARE MODERN , INTELLIGENT,'UP WITH THE TIMES'
ALTHOUGH NOT SO LONG AGO,
THEY 'D HAVE BEEN CRIMES.!
RIGHT IS NOW WRONG , CONSEQUENTLY,
WRONG'S RIGHT,
THAT'S WHAT WE'RE TOLD TODAY,
OH WHAT A PLIGHT !
SCRIPTURE HAS WARNED US THAT
THIS WOULD BE SO,
AND NATIONS, FORGETTING GOD,
WOULD BE BROUGHT LOW.
"DEAR GOD, HAVE MERCY ON OUR USA
WE NEED A REVIVAL AND FOR THIS WE PRAY.."

ELIJAH and ELISHA

One day when Elisha was ploughing a field,
The Prophet Elijah came to him and sealed
A future great ministry he would fulfill
Elijah's cloak touched him and he felt a thrill,
So when he was asked "What shall I give to you?"
Without hesitation ,Elisha just knew.

He asked for the mantle that once he had touched
For he felt the Power, now he wants twice as much!
Elijah said "This day I'll leave you and go up on high
Now don't be distracted but just keep your eye
On me, as I rise in a whirlwind & fire.
My cloak will descend and you'll have your desire".

The sons of the Prophets were gathered to view
The Epoch Event, for all of them knew
That one of their number, the cloak should receive!.
Then seeing what happened, they could not believe!
Elijah ascended, the cloak fluttered down
It totally missed them and lay on the ground!

Elisha walked boldly, the cloak to retrieve
He wrapped it around him ,for now he believed
That he, like Elijah could walk through the sea. .
He rolled up the cloak and he held it on high
"Where is the God of Elijah?" he cried.
The Jordan rolled back and he walked on dry ground !

The Sons of the Prophets, this sight did astound!
Then one of them, 'though he was awe-struck,then spoke,

"We've got the collars ,but, 'HE'S GOT THE CLOAK !'"

ENDURANCE

"Don't give up the Ship now Sailor

Don't give up the Ship!"

.That's advice that Churchill gave

With "Never, never quit!"

Although we're good at starting things

It's finishing that counts.

Success upon success we build

Until the project mounts

Into the edifice we saw

When we began the task

Our vision then was crystal clear

"What was it," do you ask?

It's reaching goals, its saving souls,

Creating things that last,

EPITAPH

MY BORROWED DUST THE EARTH MAY CLAIM

BUT I SHALL RISE IN JESUS NAME !

ETERNITY

Here on the sands of time

Do the waves eternal roll

Washing away the sand.

Savior. take my hand

Lead me to that Land

Where time cannot take

It's toll.

"Fools rush in where Angels fear to tread"
I wonder where that came from, and when it first was said.
Too bad it takes so long for some of us to learn
The truth of these old sayings, their wisdom never spurn.

One day I overheard a man I did not know too well,
He grumbled about everything –"the country's going to hell ,
The church is not performing as it should in this old world,
If we don't stop this downward trend ,into the dark we're hurled!"

On and on he went about the evils of our day
Things are not like they used to be & if he had his way,
We'd all be back. to pony and trap, oil lamps and out-house too!
The very thought of such a life sends shudders
through and through !.

" That miserable old devil!" I exclaimed, I felt so mad !
The lady next to me just smiled and said, "Oh he's my Dad !"

HE GIVETH MORE GRACE
Two verses to sing to a well-known Hymn

He openeth His hand to a world that is needy
He longeth to satisfy sinner and saint
Receive of His goodness, with manna, He'll feed thee
Then being renewed ye shall walk and not faint..

We're going one day where a River is flowing
We'll drink from those waters again and again.
And He who has given His ALL for our ransom
Will give through the ages, our life to maintain..

How priceless and Royal is Heavenly gold!
We'll walk upon Streets of it, so we are told
The values of Heaven are different from ours
The walls are of jasper with ivory towers
The gates are of pearl and the sea is as glass
The sky is so blue ,and vibrant, the grass
No tears, no more sighing, no sorrow for thee.
And there's no more death, for we'll eat from Life's Tree
It was guarded in Eden by Cherubs' flamed swords
Lest Adam partake ,disobeying God's word.

I'm glad there's a Mercy Seat made of pure gold
So we can approach God with confidence bold.
No more do the Cherubs hold swords there to guard
A sinner from seeking the mercy of God.!

IN THE DARK

The dismal Church was needing lights
The Deacons all discussed the plight..
They argued long into the night !
"A Chandelier!" said Brother Wright,
That's what we need, so let's not fight.
Then rose the Chairman of the Board ,
"A Chandelier won't please the Lord !
Now when the bill comes ,who will pay it ?
Furthermore, who's going to play it ?"
☺

"IN THE LOOP"

"We are workers together with God" 2, Corinthians 6:1

****

The Lord includes us in 'the loop' of his redemptive plan
He could have had His way without the help of unskilled man,
But in His love for humankind, He deigns to recognize
That we all need to intercede, and in that service find
A larger concept of His grace, a clearer vision of our place
In His great plan divine !

It's not His will that anyone should perish in their sin,
And so He burdens us with love so that we'll pray for them
Like Priests of old who stood before the Lord to intercede,
We too are called to boldly come and for their souls to plead.

POEM WRITTEN & READ by Heather Owen AT THE
RETIREMENT "ROAST" FOR Dr;John Phillipps who
was the Hebrew and Greek Teacher at NORTH CENTRAL
BIBLE COLLEGE (now University)

In the year of our Lord, Nineteen hundred sixteen
A boy called John Phillipps arrived on the scene.
For learning, this boy was so anxious and eager
His first baby words were "Alpha, Omega"
And fast on the heels of his talent for talking,
The neighbors exclaimed:" Look ! young Johnny is walking!"

He stretches his neck like a strangled giraffe
With it's neck in a noose, and it's dying to cough..
There's a reason for this- 'though he'd scream and he'd holler,
His Mom always pinned up his pants to his collar!
His idiosyncrasies stem from those years,
But no more of that or we'll have him in tears.

Each summer he goes to a quiet lakeside,
With Raymond Le Vang, he and Alice reside,
It's none of our business, but we'd like to know
Why, when he's up there, he just lets his beard grow,.
And lest he be fired as a Faculty member,
His whiskers are gone by the 4th of September.

You've been loved by the Faculty. Students and Staff,
For so many years, thirty four and a half.
And now you're retired you can do as you please
And grow those old whiskers clear down to your knees.
There's one further answer we all want to know
So this is the question—Here we go- (Music Department sing-)

Does John Phillipps sleep with his whiskers
Over or under the sheet?
Dos he go to bed with them tucked in his vest
And when he's asleep do they tickle his chest?
Ed Steocle, Don Meyer and Dale Berkey
Say that it has got them all beat.
Does John Phillips sleep with his whiskers,
over or under the sheet??

LIFE'S CIRCLE

Life is a circle, we're born in a bed
And usually end up there, when we are dead !
The stages of childhood , familiar become
And as we grow older we recognize some,

The things, once progressive, now go in reverse
I wonder how soon I shall be in a hearse !!
Meanwhile I'll enjoy all the fun I can get
With family and friends, food and chocolate, you bet!

It's great to be feeling alive on this earth
There's sorrow and sickness, but mostly. there's mirth.
The "Path of the Righteous" a Light ,sure will be
That shines through the years into. Eternity.

I'm thankful that I "saw the Light" in my youth
And relished the Scriptures and imbibed the Truth.
A sure foundation in Jesus I found,
The Rock of Salvation, so solid , so sound !.

LUKE 17:20

"God's Kingdom is within you" That's what the Master said.
These words He spoke to Pharisees, who spiritually were dead!
How could God's Kingdom be in men who sought an earthly King?
Did Jesus mean that somehow in the heart down deep within
Were 'Kingdom Principles' engraved by our Creator's skill,
Though buried beneath years of sin, His grace could yet reveal?

Man has a knowledge that exceeds the wisdom of this world,
He knows there's something more, somewhere
Some Treasure, some Great Pearl !

He longs to find the elusive Gem and searches far and wide,
If only he would trust in God, he'd find that Gem inside !
Why do we sweat and pulses race when doing something wrong?
Is there an inner gauge that indicates quite strong
That something's out of kilter & we're off the beaten track.?
We'd better be repentant, turn around and hurry back .

The Kingdom that's within us is a mighty driving force
That helps a person to be strong & keeps him on the course,

'Oh make us loyal subjects Lord, submitting to Your way
And we shall reign with You on earth when it's
beneath Your sway.'

The Kingdom's vast potential of the Treasure in the Field
Inspired the precious Son of God His perfect life to yield,
He paid the total price demanded to obtain the deed
Now all of it belongs to Him, that's settled and it's sealed.
The Treasure He uncovered in His earthly ministry.
He healed the sick, and raised the dead and made the blind to see
The multitudes He fed with loaves and fishes multiplied,
And then the "Kingdom Treasure" back into the Field did hide.

When Jesus comes again, the Treasure, like a panoply
Will cover all the earth just as the waters cover sea.
His Life and Health will be the right of everyone to own,
In worship and submission, all shall bow before the Throne.

At last the declaration "Peace on earth, goodwill; to men"
Will be fulfilled and we shall live in Eden once again.

MAXINE!

Maxine went out shopping with old hubby Joe;
They walked round the Mall , up and down, to and fro;
She must have tried on every shoe in the store,
'Till Joe got fed up and decided to go !

When she wasn't looking , he slipped out the door
As she took a lift to the lingerie floor,
Now after a while, so absorbed she had been
That she didn't realize Joe's not to be seen !

And so she decided to call on her 'phone
And said" Joe, now why did you leave me alone ?"
Old Joe said "Remember that Jewelry Store
Where a beautiful diamond necklace you saw?"

Her heart began pounding & then skipped a beat,
She got so excited, she could hardly speak !
"Oh Joe., there is nothing that I would want more ,
Give me five minutes, I'll be in the store."
"Now wait," he replied," We're not rich , we are poor,
I'.m just having a drink in the Tavern next door!"

MOSES

Eleven days journey-and it took them forty years!
Murmuring and complaining, not much joy but many tears!
Sick and tired of Manna which the Lord had sent from
Heaven
Wishing for the garlic and the bread that's made with leaven.

"Same old stuff" from day to day
"Moses brought us here", they say
"SMITE the Rock AGAIN and bring
Water like a Heavenly spring"

God said "To the Rock now SPEAK "
Moses, filled with rage and heat
SMOTE it ! sure ,the water came
But now Moses was to blame.

Christ's the Rock that followed them-
. Only once the Lamb was slain.
' Stricken Rock with streaming side'
Type of Christ ONCE crucified.

Destiny, the Lord had planned
Milk and honey- Promised Land!
Moses did not enter in
For that SECOND strike was sin.

God recalled his ancient prayer
On the Mount Moses was there.
He saw the Glory of the Lord.
In spite of Satan's threatening word.

"The Lord rebuke you" Michael said
And brought him from "The Realms of Dead"
To answer that deep-rooted cry-
"Show me Thy glory' ere I die"

Ex15:24. Num,14:2,29&,16:41&116
Ex.17:6& 20:8 I.Cor:10:2 Ex:40:35&33:18
Jude 9

MOVE THE ROCKS

Those heavy rocks that come to view & so obstruct the way !
Does some satanic person put them there from day to day ?
There's fertile soil beneath them, but we can sow no seed
Until the rocks are rolled aside, then nothing will impede
The sprouting of those living Seeds, in due time, shoots will show
And in that fertile soil that feeds them, you will see them grow.

Oh seeking soul, you find it strange that God LOVES me and you
When earthquakes & volcanoes seem to contradict what's true!
If you will roll those "rocks" aside ,& leave them there for now
The Word of God will take firm root ,& God will show you how
To rise above objections, 'though sensible they sound,
And new Life from the precious Seed of God's Word will abound.

NICE TRY!

"J.H" saw the Dr: for Lisa, his wife.

She'd not see a Dr:-no not on your life!

"Oh I'll have no Dr: push poke me and prod,

For I have unusual respect for my bod!"

******

The Dr: examined J,H. on the table,

He asked for his symptoms so he would be able

To diagnose just what his 'illness' would be

He gave Lisa's symptoms ,as if he were she!

*****

Now off home he went to meet Lisa's reception.

She asked for the pills and the Dr's direction

J.H. sat down carefully, "No pills have I got"

He sighed "No prescription-.he gave me a shot!"

No need to climb the mountain peak
To hear the Lord almighty speak,
He said that He'd come down !
And this He did and in a crib
Of sheep and oxen's straw
He came, with glory veiled in flesh
And He was God, for sure!

The Angels all rejoiced to see
The Word revealed to man
In language they could understand,
That was the eternal plan.

Divested of His attributes
Contented now to be
God's "Second Man" who would retrieve
What Adam lost
At awful cost,
In paradise, with Eve,

The Better Covenant He made
With His own Blood was sealed,
By His free will
He did fulfill
The Law, at Sinai given.

Now Grace and Truth in Christ abound
So all may be forgiven.

NOISE

It seems young folks can't get enough
Of beating drums and guitars strummed
But when they reach old age,
They'll find their hearing is impaired
And things don't sound the same.
And they will then remember
That they have themselves to blame.
Because the old folks told them
To turn the sound down lower
But NO, they loved the rhythmic beat,
The vibration and power
Of sound waves beating on their chest.
Some day they'll find that "Mom knew best"
The 'happy clappy' took it's toll,
The heavy metal ,rock 'n roll
Demand a price be paid.
And now what can those deaf ones do
But wear a hearing aid?!

ONE MORE MOVE

The enemy said "checkmate!" but the King has one more move!
Trust Him to have the answer, and His great wisdom prove,
Because it is " unsearchable, His ways past finding out"
The finished work at Calvary leaves naught for one to doubt.
No human wisdom touched that height,
nor plumbed its untold depth;
We do not understand the scope the height, the length, the breadth,
For as by one man sin came in, and doomed the human race,
So by God's Son He has released a flood of endless Grace.
"Checkmate, be gone!" for Christ has won,
the King has made the move!
And that's Redemption's wondrous plan,
God's wisdom here to prove.

****

Every year in Europe a Chess Competition is arranged
They play against a back-drop of a painting that depicts Satan
looking smug as the man across the table has his head in his
hands defeated. Underneath is written: -

"CHECKMATE"
One day famous a player gazed at the painting for a longtime,
then broke the silence with a shout—

"THE KING HAS ONE MORE MOVE !!"

YES !!!!

120

OUR SCHOOL TEACHERS

Every day that they work.

They are on the alert

For some deranged fool

Who might come to the school

And scare all the children to death.,

It's time to bring back

To our schools, what they lack

.Let's forget protocol

And consider the souls

Of our kids, and ask God to protect..

Return to God's Word,

For the children deserve

To hear about God's saving Grace,

For who knows what they'll face

In this world where such evil abounds!

****

Note:-
The Bible is banned from our schools
but permitted in Prison !

PASSING ELEGANCE

Down through the arches of the years ,with confidence and grace,
She walks with poise and dignity and clear unpainted face.
Her dress, attractive in its style, yet modest in appeal,
Her shoes support her dainty feet, without a six inch heel'!

We stand in awe, sometimes disgust at what we see today,
Our kids pay cash for junk that we, for sure, would throw away
I'm thankful that fads come and go, like tides on ocean main,
Let's hope the next big wave that breaks brings elegance again!

PENETCOST

Luke tells us in the Book of Acts

Some very interesting facts

That happened in the early Church

Who thought they'd been left in the lurch

When Jesus went on high.

Then they remembered He had said

That when He'd leave for Heaven

Another Comforter from God the Father would be given

And so they waited fifty days

To get their hearts' desire

Then power from Heaven came to them

Like Wind and tongues of Fire.

PIZZA DILEMMA

I'll not get Pizza there again,

I know I asked for simply "plain"

But there should be some sauce and cheese.

Did they do this just for a tease?

I picked the phone up and I dialed

The Pizza , man ,and to him riled

"I opened up the Box " I said

And found there's nothing there but bread! "

"THAT CANNOT BE" the man replied,

"SAUCE CHEESE AND GARLIC ON THE SIDE,

THAT'S HOW IT OUGHT TO BE!"

"Oh— —sorry Sir,—I must confess—

The box is in an awful mess—

The Pizza's upside down!"

QUESTION

What did the pork chop say to the steak?

ANSWER.

"Moo, moo, moo,

I wish that I were you.

I think that I could fake

That I'm a New York steak,

Then I could go to Jewish Picnics too!

There'd be no greater thrill

Than to sizzle on the grill,

And have a Rabbi choose ME over YOU !."

Question:-

WHY DID THE HUNGRY DINASAW CROSS THE ROAD?

Answer-
Because he saw a diner!

Restoration

God picks up the pieces and puts them together
Adhering them fast with his grace.
For every believer who truly repents
He frees him from sin and disgrace.

The vessel, once lovely in shape and design
Was battered and broken by sin,
But God, as a Craftsman of infinite skill
.Restorative work will begin
He'll make it again, even though it was marred,
It still is held fast in His hand
And one day that vessel restored and transformed
Will be there in that heavenly land.
The Angels will stare in amazement to see
What redemptive skill has achieved.
The "manifold wisdom' and infinite grace
He'll establish through those who believed
Ephesians 3:10 Jeremiah 18;

ST JOHN 2::7-10

"Fill the jars with water"
They filled them to the brim!
That was beyond obedience
To what was asked of them .
If only 'to the neck 'was filled,
In case some water would be spilled.
Then only that much it would yield
In 'new-created wine'
Obedience to the full extent
Is our desire and our intent ,
Let's go the extra mile .

.And pray God helps us do just that,
And do it with a smile!

The lesson is, to give to Christ all that we have and are,
In full surrender we would be like that full water jar
And in the Hands of Him who made the grapes upon the vine,
He'll by-pass natural law,
And turn the water into wine.

STRANGER IN CHURCH

One Sunday night the Sermon ended,
All the people who attended
Bowed their heads and waited for
"The Blessing" that they'd heard before.
Suddenly we looked above,
Was it a snow-white flying Dove?
Oh no! It was a big black BAT.
In Church!! What do you think of that?
.Brooms and buckets quickly sought
From the basement they were brought
Deacons jumping up on pews,
Did, to say the lease, amuse!
When they got him, I don't know
If the Deacons let him go.
All I know is, Sunday next,
When the Preacher read the text,
That familiar sound was heard,
And we saw that "evil bird"
Zooming over every seat like he did the other week
Brooms and buckets to the fore, "Brother Bill, open the door!"
"Mrs Deacon" has a plan- simply call the Orkin man.!!
(duh!)

SUNDAY SCHOOL ANNIVERSARY.

To Sunday School a Speaker came
Dr' Fred Crisp was his name,
Each year he came, and every time
He brought an object,- his design
..
One year he brought a great big book,
The children took a second look !
Four feet high and two feet wide-
We wondered what could be inside !

Well, soon he showed us what was there,
A library of books quite rare,
For from each one there fell a picture
Of a story found in Scripture.

Joined they were with scarlet cord
Signifying that God's Word
Is all about Redemption's Plan
How God would rescue fallen man.

We never will forget the tale
Of Jonah, three days in a whale !
And Jericho, whose walls fell down
When Israelites all marched around.

He started out with Adam's sin,
The serpent, then God's offering,
And ended with triumph through grace
How all may see God face to Face.

It gave us all a sense of awe
That we had never known before
We learned that we should "read mark, learn'
And God's plan for our lives discern.

TEEMED UP

☺

"Hawk-Eye Joe" who had dementia
Thought to Golf Links he would venture.
Teeming up with "Long-Ball Bill"
They would play on Crystal Hill.
'Hawk-Eye" had the greatest vision,
He could see with fine precision
Just exactly where balls landed
But did not play single-handed.
Sometimes he would get confused,
Wondering which iron to use.
"Long-Ball Bill" sent his ball high,
Very high into the sky!
"Hawk-Eye, where did that one go ?"
"I CAN SEE IT, YES , KNOW!"
Past the sand trap, past the green;
Not a sign of it was seen!
"Where'd it go Joe? My best shot?"
"SORRY 'LONG BALL' I FORGOT!"

☺

THE EVERGREEN TREE

Those cone shaped verdant sentinels that line our avenue
Add beauty to the landscape and pleasure to the view.
We cut them down at CHRISTMAS time
and to our homes we bring,
Adding trinkets and the Star, "Oh Tannenbaum" we sing.

Although they're green throughout the year
And bring to us some winter cheer,
New life does not come until Spring
And then we see a lovely thing!
At EASTER new growth comes in sight
It seems to happen overnight,
Each branch, a tiny cross will sprout !
It took a friend to point that out !
I'd never noticed until then,
How blind was I to comprehend
That there's a message in that tree,
Repeating it to you and me;
From top and sides and all around
The crosses tell new life abounds
.

With evergreens we celebrateThe birth and death of He
Who through the Cross Salvation gives to you & gives to me.

THE BOOMERANG

Be good to yourself, don't harbor a grudge;
Just practice forgiveness, let God be the Judge;
For bitter resentment, you'll pay a big price
GET OVER IT ! make up your mind to be nice !

There's many a person who goes to a "Shrink"
When all that they need is to change how they think.
Step back and observe what your attitudes are
Towards other folks you may think are bizarre!

If you point at someone who's " fallen from grace,"
Three fingers point back at you,- so hide your face!!
Condemn someone when you don't know all the facts
Is just like a boomerang—that's how it acts!

THE CHURCH CLOCK

This old clock will tell the story
Of the Church's former glory—

"Oh I saw how people praised
With their hands to Heaven raised.
Preachers seldom looked my way
In case the time had slipped away.
They would preach until the Lord
Would bless them and conform the Word.
Prophesies came many-a-time,
Mrs Wells gave one in rhyme!
That surprised me, and the shock
Made my' tick' go tick, tock tock!
How I wish that I could chime
And express this joy of mine.
I can only say 'Tick Tock'

For I'm just the old church clock."

1941 "Some where in England"

The Church was bombed in world War Two,
The members wondered what to do
For it would take a while before
They'd get it fixed from roof to floor.
The steeple too, had fallen down
And lay in pieces on the ground.
There was a Pub across the Street,
The Bartender said they could meet
And have church Service there.
The only thing they could not move
Was Polly Parrot who would 'groove'
Whenever music played!
Well Sunday came and everyone
Seemed happy with their new Church home.
The Preacher wasn't all that free,
When Polly squawked out "New M,C.!"
The Choir then entered row by row,
And Polly shouted "New Floor Show!"
And then the Parrot, looked around
And she shouted very loud
"HERE THEY ARE, THE SAME OLD CROWD!"

THE CUP OF BLESSING.

I'm drinking from the saucer, for my cup has overflowed!
God promised He would meet my needs
while on this earthly road,

But He has more than satisfied the thirsting of my soul
His blessings are immeasurable, and stretch from pole to pole.

We cannot calculate the size of God's great gifts galore,
He gives from the abundance of His vast and bounteous store.

Enough for all mankind He gives,
It is His will that all shall live.

Oh I would do my part to hold the cup to parch-ed lips
Rejoicing then to see the souls reviving as they sip.

And deepest needs of dying man may then be satisfied
And we, who hold the cup shall find, we too,
have been revived!

"THE HOLE"

Off to Boy's Camp Johnnie went
A real good time was his intent,
And that, he had, for every day
A team was chosen, and he'd play.
*****

His very best he gave to it,
Then one day, whoops! he heard a split!
It was his fancy denim jeans
And they were splitting at the seams
*****

"Oh dear" he thought." my mother bought
These jeans ,but they are not for sport!
And now just look what I have done!'
And then he heard a call "Hey John!"
* ****

It was the Counselor who called,
He thought that she was going to scold,
But, no, she took him ,and his jeans
She mended on her 'stitch machine'
*****

And while she sewed, to Johnny showed
The way of full Salvation.
And he believed, & Christ received
And was a 'new creation'.
*****

That night at Campus Church they met,
And Johnnie hoped that he would get
A chance to tell of his ordeal
And how he found the Savior real..
*****

The Preacher spoke about the man
Who had to make a different plan
And came a most unusual way
To meet the Savior on that day.
*****

Down through the roof he came with hopes
He was let down with 2 strong ropes
A hole was made to facilitate
A man in such a sickly state.
*****

Then Johnny called (he almost screams!)
"I met Jesus thru' a hole in my jeans!"

THE NEW PASTOR

We voted for a Pastor who could preach and teach and pray,
He met all the requirements of the Board which met Tuesday.
To get us more acquainted , we invited him to be
Our honored guest who'd come with us when fishing on the sea.

*****

Well off we sailed, all six of us ,delighted with the thought
That we were with the Pastor, even if no fish were caught.
Now we'd just started out to sea,
When Deacon Joe said "Oh dear me!"
"What's wrong ?" enquired the other bunch,
"It's in the car,—I left my lunch!"
"Well that's OK" the Preacher said,
"I know your car, it's two-tone red,
I'll get it, just give me the key"
So out he stepped ON to the sea!
We all were shocked to watch him walk
Too stunned we were, to even talk!

Then spoke the Chairman of the Board-
"Was it the leading of the Lord?

I can't believe we voted in
A Pastor who can't even swim!"

138

THE PUMPKIN

I think I'm like a pumpkin that was chosen from the batch,

Was washed & trimmed and freed from dirt
I'd picked up from the patch.

Then put through quite a process of digging out the seeds

Of anger, critism, and of jealousy and greed,

Then I was cut and fashioned to the Craftsman's own design

God put His Light within me and He said, "Now let it shine!"

The Salvation Army "Open Air Meeting" 1933.

At 3 o'clock the Comrades meet
Outside a Pub on Brixton Street.
The Captain steps into the ring
To read a verse before we sing.

The 'band' consists of three violins
Two cornets & a big bass drum.
We hope that other folk will come
To join our feeble few.

The sound- such as you've never heard
Was worse than any funeral dirge,
My Dad was really quite concerned,
And wondered if poor Al had learned
To play in any key but C.
He glanced across at Albert's book
And had to take a second look
He's on a different page!!

Then brother Burgess ,with violin
Stepped into the ring to sing
"The devil and me we can't agree
Glory hallelujah!
I hate him and he hates me,
Glory Hallelujah!"

He then began a tale to tell.
How God had saved his soul from Hell.
"Gospel Shots" were fired next,
So we shouted Gospel Texts,
Then the Captain closed in prayer.
And so ends our 'Open Air'

THE TALKING TEA POT

"Hello, dear friends, I have met you before,
When into your tea cups, my brown brew was poured.

There's many a gossip I've heard at the table
I know you are pleased that I'm really not able

To spread any further the stories I hear
I bury them deep in my tea leaves for fear

That they will get out and be scattered around
Then someone that's guilty at last will be found.

O friends, learn a lesson from this old tea pot,
Don't talk about others and think that you're not

As guilty as they are, perhaps even worse!
Remember tale-bearers are under a curse!

But that's not the end of my message to you,
I have heard some good things and know they are true,

I've poured out my tea into many a cup
Reviving the drooping, and made them lookup.

Reviving is really what I'm all about,
And that's what I do so tea pours out my spout.

My mission accomplished1 how happy I am
That you enjoyed tea with your doughnuts and jam.."

The Train & The Tresses

Like every morning—nothing new
I board the train to Waterloo.
As usual, no one ever talks,
Then "Blondie" on the platform walks,
Gets in, flops down upon the seat
And for a moment, our eyes meet.

She flipped unruly hair and said
"Last night before I went to bed
I washed my hair in something new,
A soapless blond high-light shampoo
I cannot keep it off my face,
Today it will not stay in place!"

A moment later, off she goes
And tells again, her shampoo woes,
"Last night," she said, I washed my hair
And now it's flying everywhere"
I'm smiling, trying to be nice,
But if that woman said it twice,
She said it fifty times!

Thank God, I thought, we'll soon be there,
I'm tired of hearing about hair!

As we rolled into Waterloo
A fellow who was fed up too
Got up to go,-trod on her toe,
And just before he did alight
Said "Sorry Dear, the reason's clear,

I WASHED MY FEET LAST NIGHT!"

143

The Tweet: ☺

The tweet around the world was heard

Was it a rare humungous bird

Sent from the Vatican?

Oh no! the Newsman said last week

The Pope sent out a Papal Tweet.

A Big red bird should tweet his 'say'

That is a Cardinal's forte!

So now I vote," demote the Pope

So he can tweet away"

THE WEB.

The ancient Celts of Druid Priests were hiding in a cave
Lest they would be enslaved and tortured due to enemy rage.
They prayed for their protection from the enemy at large
Surrendered to the will of God and asked Him to take charge.
They thought that God might do some cataclysmic act
To prove that He is God and they should all believe the fact.
But as the time went on, they watched a most amazing thing,
A spider, by the open door , began a web to spin.
God's ways are far above what our small minds
could 'ere conceive,
For who would guess, a spider, God would designate to weave
A web to stretch above the door, from top
to reach down to he floor?
And as the enemy approached, seeing the web,
the Captain spoke ,
"Don't bother to inspect that cave, no Druids are in there
For there's a perfect spider's web more fine than human hair,
And if some Druids went inside,
Thinking that from us they'd hide,
The web would not be there intact.
So let's not waste more time on that !"
Who'd guess a spider's web would save
Those Druids from the Romans' rage ?

A SPINSTER'S FUNERAL

Old Annie was a single gal, and oh, so proud to be,

A ninety year old woman boasting of virginity!

Her life would soon be over, & Eternity 'twould be,

And so she bought a grave lot in a near-by cemetery.

She chose the Funeral hymns, the Preacher,

those she knew so well

Who'd glowing eulogies recite to prove she's not in Hell!

The Pall-Bearers were chosen too, all women from her Town,

And she would lie embalmed, and in a snow white satin gown.

The Clergy said," That's not the way, a Funeral to perform,

Men should be Bearers of the casket, Annie, that's the norm."

Well Annie was indignant, and to the Clergy said

"No man took *me* out while alive; they won't when I am dead!"

BE STILL

Be still, be still, be still
Until
You will see how the matter will fall

Let patience have her perfect work in you,
Just trust the One who guides
He will see you through,
Be still, be still, be still,
Until
You shall see how the matter will fall.

Ruth 3.28 KJV

BEYOND

There's a song beyond the silence, there's a whisper in the winds,
And there's an oratorio that every ocean sings.
There's laughter beyond labor, and joy beyond our tears,
"Forever" is not counted by our calendar of years.
We only see the shadows and the substance is concealed,
We know some day that all will be revealed.
The mysteries unfathomed, when surfaced, will amaze,
The learned men, who'll then confess, "It was revealed to babes."
There is a Spirit deep within that knows when something's true,
The "natural man" can't understand, he doesn't have a clue!
But to the one who seeks to know His ways, He will impart,
Knowledge of the truth that he can hide within his heart.
We'll hear the song, the whisper, and the oratorio,
The laughter that will joy express and stem the tears that flow.
Eternity's behind all time, and in the great Beyond,
So praise the Lord and shout for joy, we'll sing redemption's song!

CHANGING TIMES

The Artist's paint brush prophesies
A time when women have three eyes!
They are so horribly misshapen.
That for monsters are mistaken
Now we look at frogs and find
Extra legs ,it blows the mind'
We've so polluted air and water
That genetic codes are altered.
Hormones in our food injected ,
Masculinity's rejected!
Men stay home, the kids to mind,
Wives go out, a job to find.

I took a trip into the Louvre,
I just had a point to prove,— — — — —
'Ancient artistry still lives,
Never changes, and forgives
The modern travesties'
But, oh great Scott!—that's what I feared— —
Mona Lisa's grown a beard!

149

Christ is You, the Hope of Glory

"That Christ be fully formed in you," was Paul's desire and plea:
We say "Oh Lord! amazing this, tell me, how can it be?"
The answer we can't understand, it is a mystery!
The Virgin, body, heart and soul were to the Spirit given
Miraculous conception then took place, so it is written
She magnified the God of her Salvation with her voice,
Her spirit too, in God her Savior caused her to rejoice.

As time went by, she knew the stigma of that great decision,
Misunderstanding and disgrace because of her condition.
But in God's time her vindication came at Cana's feast
When into wine the water turned, by Christ the Great High Priest.
Now let the Spirit work in you, whatever is His plan
And "Christ in you, the only Hope" will make you His new man.

CONCORDANCES DEFINED

YOUNGS is for the young STRONGS for the strong
CRUDENS for the crude

****

STRONGS is for the mighty ones who feel they are mature
And they are Christian soldiers who hardships can endure,

For those who're Pentecostal, and who speak in other tongues
Well, they would use the newer one,
& look things up in YOUNGS

CRUDENS is the ancient one,-granddaddy of them all
That's where we looked up 'naughty words'
when we were three feet tall!

Now when we're going to teach a class selecting words to speak,
If we don't like the meaning, we'll just look it up in Greek!

As if that's going to help the folks who're English to the core
Don't let's think we re scholarly, we're nothing but a bore!!!

Easter

The wonder of the empty tomb has shattered history!
It caused the realms of death to quake. O glorious victory!
The Devil stood on awe to see the Man once crucified
Come from the grave, a world to save, and death and hell defy.
The conquering Savior used the key
To set the long-held captives free,
Led them to Paradise and then
He left Heaven's Gates ajar for men
And all may enter in!

Hampstead Bible School Motto

Lord keep this wonderful truth in my mind,

'While in Thy service, true pleasure I find,

Let me love Jesus more fervently than

The joy that He gives while fulfilling His plan.,

———⊶⊷———

Howard Carter wrote the first verse.::-

I am free from condemnation,

What a full and free salvation.

We have light and revelation,

From all sin emancipation,

Through the precious blood.

"Child of God" now, what a wonder !

Satan's fetters loosed asunder!

Jesus builds a Mansion yonder,

On this blessed thought I ponder,

He'll return for me!

He Purifies Like Fire

He purifies like fire—refreshes like the rain,

Gives fragrance like the lily—balm of Gilead for our pain.

He's gentle like the snow white dove—.a Lamb that has been slain.

The Lion of Judah, who some day the whole world will reclaim,

He is the heavenly Shepherd; He'll not lose one single lamb,

But seek until He finds him, He is the great I AM

And His will is that none be lost, and that will be fulfilled,

In spite of man's transgressions and in spite of his free will.

He is the Door, through which all men shall ultimately pass,

He is the Light that lighted every man from first to last.

He cannot be defeated, when such a price He paid

And all the sin of all the world upon His heart was laid

His mercy and enduring Love can put His grace on hold

If that need be, until the last lost sheep is in the Fold!

154

Joseph

There's a right, & there's a wrong way to evaluate ourselves,
Joseph, with some self-esteem in his ancestry delved
Great grand father was ABRAHAM & God called him His Friend,
To his son, ISAAC, God affirmed that blessings would extend
For generations, & to all the families of the earth.
Now JACOB saw the Birthright to be something of great worth,
And that belonged to Esau, but he sold it to his twin,
The Birthright, Jacob now possessing,
knew that he should get the blessing
It belonged to him.
The way it happened was not right; if only they had waited
In God's good time He would have got what he anticipated.
Jacob became ISRAEL up on the mountain height.
An Angel wrestled with him and he put up such a fight
That finally the Angel had to cripple him to crown,
A Prince with God' he then became, a man of great renown.
And he was JOSEPH'S father, no wonder that he said
"Oh how can I this sin commit, to Potiphar she's wed!"
His heritage was godly and his past without a stain,
He came from pit to palace, from prison, then to fame
He kept the faith he had been taught, and valued his good name.
For faithfulness, forgiveness & for his wisdom clear
To him was given the title of "Lord Zaphenath-Paanea"

LATEST GRIPE

Reluctantly we've settled for the ever-changing time
For "poetry" that's awful, without rhythm, sense or rhyme!
And "tunes" (if one can call them such)–
five notes in repetition,
"Till I am bored out of my mind and pray for some remission!
I think that Wesley, Isaac Watts and godly men who gave
Their near-immortal artistry, would now turn in their grave
If they could hear the travesty that's recognized these days
As modern and contemporarily worship prayer and praise.

Leslie Weatherhead

"Gash the earth with your railway cutting,& nature at once gets busy on the scar & covers it with not only the green grass which grows on surrounding fields, but with tender violets & primroses which would not grow until a cleft in the earth provided shelter from the north winds(From "The Will of God" by Leslie Weatherhead)

The earth-removing monster clawed & turned

The emerald undulations & it churned

The tender ferns, the heather & the heath

Their softened hues & beauty ploughed beneath.

A railway line was laid in stark relief!

A season passed since from our window pane

We saw the first of many-a- rumbling train.

Now, in that hillside deeply gashed & torn

Sweet primroses & violets have been born

Awake, my soul, it is a glorious morn!

My Belief

I believe,'tho we do not yet see all things beneath His feet,

Yet by faith we see Christ crowned and occupy

Heaven's highest seat.

All the kingdoms of this world shall then become

The Kingdom of the Anointed One,

Prince of Peace, Prince of peace!

I believe there'll come a day when at his feet all men shall bow,

And He'll take His rightful crown from off His Head.

His pierced brow,

And while Angels stand in breathless awe around

And ransomed Choirs burst into sound,

He will yield, He will yield

All the Kingdoms, crowns tiaras diadems, into the Hand

Of the Father, who has trusted him to win from every land

And from every kindred, tribe & people rare,

A spotless Bride in garments fair,

All, this. Praise God, I believe!

Parental Responsibility

"It takes a Village to raise a child!"

That's what I heard,

It's quite absurd!

Just let a Village do your work

While you, parental duty shirk.

That way THEY take the praise or blame

For what the outcome is.

Now if your child becomes a crook

It's not YOUR fault it's what THEY taught ,

And you are "off the hook!"

PHONE TALK

I am here for you to use
Night or day as you shall choose
Pick me up- your faithful phone
I'll greet you with my dialing tone!
B flat is what you hear from me,
I sing that back piano key!
And now you dial or punch my keys
I listen while you 'shoot the breeze'
And wonder what you find to say
For hours on end, from day to day.
My patience gone! I've done my best
Please put me down and let me rest!

Prosperity Gospel

New babies will cry and they'll make such a fuss,
Until we will give them just what they want from us.
God is like that to the brand new believers
Who know nothing else but to be big receivers.
Soon things will change and the real world they'll face.
"Prosperity Gospel's not always the case!
If, soon after sowing the harvest would grow
We'd all be 'spoilt rotten' and rolling in dough!
We'll wait for the season of reaping to come
And we'll give again, but next time, we'll keep some!

SLOW DOWN

Travel in the fast lane, and you'll miss a lot of things,
Slow down and watch the sparrow and see the fledgling's wings

As fluttering, he tries to fly and rise up from the ground.
He hears the distant chirping of his mother, and the sound
Inspires the little creature to try his skill at flight
And so he flaps his tiny wings and tries with all his might.

Then off he goes, the battle's won, he's conquered gravity!
The thrill of flying high is his and new found sights to see.
Slow down oh busy "Martha"; life's fraught with many-a-care,
"Come ye yourselves apart" said Christ,
and spend some time in prayer,
Like Mary, choose "that better part", sit at His feet and learn,
You'll get a new perspective and His perfect will discern.

THE GIVER

The Giver of life died that all men might live,

He gives just because it's His nature to give,

Distributing out of His bountiful store,

He gives us so much, yet He has so much more.

O manifold mercy, abundance of grace!

He causes the sun to shine in every place,

The gentle rain falls on the good & the ill

The Father decreed it, for that is His will.

He opens His hand to a world in great need,

He'll satisfy us and our spirits will feed

There's manna from Heaven that falls like the rain

And we can receive it again and again.

We're going someday, where a clear river's flowing,

We'll drink from that water again and again.

And He who has given His all, for my ransom

Will give through the ages my life to maintain.

ABERFAN DISASTER

The years have passed, black dust has settled;

White arches stand out stark against the blue sky.

Their shape bespeaks of rainbows bringing hope,

In contrast to the cold white color of death.

Innocent children shrouded in a cloak of merciless slag,

Died in hope of a glorious resurrection,

In robes of white,when the trumpet sounds.

In 1966 a mountain of slag from the coal pits of South Wales slid and covered a Schoolhouse of 200 children with their teachers .

Bereaved

There is a sorrow that mere words cannot express,

Nor tears relieve that painful suffering and distress.

Time helps us cope with sorrow and with change,

We slowly learn our lives to rearrange,

And in our loss find gain.

If that sounds heartless, give me some alternative,

With which to live, and sanity maintain.

BERNIE THE BATON BOY

Old Bernie had an orchestra of nine or ten old chaps,
They'd never had a lesson, (well, one or two, perhaps)!
Now Bernie'd been a passionate Conductor in his prime,
He tried to teach them how to read the notes & keep in time.
His teaching was to no avail,
For every one of them would fail,
to get the sound just right.

He's like a windmill on a hill,
You'd swear he took a steroid pill.!
His arms and legs flay every way -
A good contortionist, I'd say!

He lost his baton and dropped dead!
The Mayo Clinic Doctor said.
They found the baton, it was stuck
In poor old Bernie's lower gut!

They buried him with his baton,
And now he's singing in" kingdom come."

"But if not—" Daniel 3:18

'THE ANSWER' is to big for puny human minds to grasp

And so He veils it from our eyes although in faith we ask..

In mercy, we are shielded from the Truth that's so profound

From Light that would our eyes impair and

throw us to the ground!.

He is the Truth, He is the Light ,He also is the Way.

We trust Him 'though we cannot see ,and plod on day by day.

The greatest faith that we can have,is like three men of old

Who in the fiery furnace went, and came forth like pure gold..

Their faith held strong, as through the air those

Hebrew boys were thrown

God's Son, they met, in flames of fire!

IF ONLY THEY HAD KNOWN !

Had they, from Time stepped for a while, into Eternity

And seen the Eternal Son of God 'ere His Nativity ?

Calvary's Mountain

Capture a vision of Calvary's Mountain,
That's where the precious Son of God expired for me.
His sacred Blood has created a fountain.
And since I plunged beneath its flow, I am set free.

Free from the thralldom of sin's dread dominion
Brought into new relationship with Christ my Lord.
Gone are my proud and my lofty opinions ,
Now I shall live for Jesus, trusting in His Word.

CANADIAN GEESE

Year after year they circle round
In droves, and settle on the ground.
All decked in snow-white 'bibs' they seek
For worms or anything to eat.

Here they come, another bunch
Looking for a Fairway Lunch.
Just as they, their repast start -
"Wow ! here comes a golfer's cart!"

They walk, they run and then they fly
Up and away into the sky.
But soon they're back, and on the track,
Having yet another snack.

They enjoy the Fairway Food
So I guess it must be good!
For they come back every fall
In spite of the unwelcome ball!

They're getting 'geared up' for the flight
That they will take one Autumn night
It is a sight! Oh my! Oh my!
THREE HUNDRED GEESE TAKE TO THE SKY!

They're going South to warmer clime
So say "Goodbye, until next time."

Culturally Blind

Don't let our western culture blind us to a broader view.

God's bigger than the customs that were taught to me and you.

We learn the language "Christianese" and think it is 'of God' !

We're "People of the Book", you know,

our Churches simply do not grow,

We're DRY, but onward plod!,,,,,,,,

Now "where are all the miracles our fathers told us of?

And where are prophets and apostles,?

Where's the LIVING God?"

Like Pharisees of old. we're trapped in customs and set ways,

No room for change or new ideas, we have to satisfy our peers

And harp on 'good old days!

DANGER AND DELIGHT

I heard the most unearthly noise and wondered 'What the heck!'
And then I saw that someone shot a golf ball on my deck.
I almost heard the words "It wasn't I who hit your screen"
As he, the cart drove swiftly by, hoping I had not seen!
There's lots of fun in living on a Golf Course, that's well known,
But who'd have thought my sunny deck would be
a Golf War zone?
I watched the well-clad gentleman take many-a-practice stroke
And then ,with an almighty swing he hit it. what a joke!
The ball went high into the sky and landed in the sand!
I stood out on the deck and laughed then gave him 'a good hand'.

EMPATHY

Just listen to me, do not lecture
Don't give reasons or conjecture,
I don't need a special reason.
I just want an arm to lean on.

Lend a sympathetic ear.
Let me see your falling tear.
That speaks volumes to my heart,
Understanding does impart
More than words can 'ere express
Can be given by a kiss!

Exploration

There's all eternity to spend exploring outer space,

I wonder why men have to try to find another race,

They want to feel they're not alone in this vast universe

And want to prove that someone's there to bless us, not to curse,

Is it that human instinct that's aware of God above?

And does man look for someone else, or something else to love/

It will not satisfy the constant nagging at the mind

To land upon another sphere and there, only to find

An empty, lifeless lump of rock rotating round the sun,

How disappointing, for he thought he'd find how life began.

Why are we always seeking something that's beyond our ken?

The Bible tells us how it all began and how 'twill end.

And we'll not find what we are seeking there, or o the earth

No matter what we try to do, so just give up the search!

Jehovah Jireh

Though the fig tree does not blossom,

and there's no fruit on the vine,

Yet Jesus still 'turns water into wine

Although the 'fridge is empty and the food cupboard is bare

Jehovah Jireh will provide and give enough to spare.

The widow in obedience gave all she had away

But never lacked in oil or meal from that momentous day.

Sometimes God tests and tries our faith,and we encounter lack,

So by his grace, establish faith in God, and don't look back.

A GOLF BALL'S LAMENT

My sphere severely dented, like pimples inside out!

I suffered there in silence, & did not dare to shout,.

I knew that preparation was a necessary thing

If I would ever be in flight like eagles on the wing.

I dreamed of flying high above the fairway to the green

And men would peer into the sky amazed at what they'd seen.,

For I was almost lost amid a nimbostratus cloud

And heard the shouts of "Well played Sir"

that rose up from the crowd.

Then in the cup I ended up, but to my great dismay,

I woke up in a Sporting Store with others on display!

St. Andrews, oh St. Andrews, how I'd dreamed of being struck

By some man in a funny skirt, some Scottish "mucky-muck!"

But I would have to settle for just mediocre thrills

And never see St Andrews, but just play on Crystal Hills.

LIFE AND TRUTH

Life wanders through the Halls of Science, unidentified.
They probe into her ancestry but are not satisfied.
I wonder why they can't accept the explanation given
In chapter 1 o Genesis, how God made Earth and Heaven.

And from the dust of planet Earth
He fashioned man and gave him worth
With His own Breath Divine.

There'll come a time when Scientists who really Truth have sought
Will realize that Christians, who God's own Word have taught
Had grasped by faith, the facts that now are dawning on their mind
And LIFE and TRUTH personified in Jesus Christ will find.

Losing our Identity

We're losing our identity as Christians in this world
The USA and Europe are quickly being hurled
Into a state of nonchalance where nothing matters much
Except the trivial pursuit of sport events and such!
The Media distorts the truth in interest of itself
As long as nobody protests and they can gain more wealth.

Destroying values once held dear, and in their place to bring
A sense that everything's alright, the future's in good hands!
The president will fix it all, he is a super-man!
You "do your thing and be yourself and just do what feels good"
And never mind those "fuddy-duddies" who, in good faith would
These modern notions overturn, restoring what is right.
We need a change, that is quite clear, so just stay in the fight.

Lunar Phase

Lunar phase command the wave
The tides on every shore1
The sun will rise, the sun will set
As always, in the east and west
And these are facts for sure!

There is a cosmic order set
"Tis wondrous in our eyes,
It always was, and will be yet
'Till Jesus cleaves the skies
And comes again on Earth to reign.
Be ready, and be wise!

MISSIONARY TO DEATH'S DOMAIN.

Christ fulfilled a mission to the place of Death,
Encountered every saint and seer-
All who had lived and had died in faith
Waiting for Messiah to appear,

"WHAT ARE YOU WAITING FOR ABEL?
YOU PLEASED TO LORD WITH OFFERINGS"
"Oh I'm waiting for the One of whom 'tis said
'His Blood speaketh better things'"

"WHAT ARE YOU WAITING FOR ABRAHAM.?
YOU LEFT ALL YOUR IDOLS BEHIND,
YOU SERVED THE LIVING GOD FOR MANY_ YEAR
NOW WHAT DO YOU HOPE TO FIND?"

"I'm looking for a Son from Heaven,"
I'm ready now for Paradise
I lifted up my eyes from Moriah
And, by faith I saw The Sacrifice

"WHAT ARE YOU WAITING FOR MALACHAI
WITH YOUR EYES UPON THE EASTERN SKIES?"
"There has been a night of gloom.
But the morning's coming soon
And I'm waiting for the Sun to rise!"

Many were the saints He encountered there,
All the stories, time would fail to tell,
But Jesus smote the Devil in his own domain
And took the keys of Death and Hell.

Mighty Jesus! Risen Jesus!
He, the captives led to Paradise.
"His Blood speaks better things"
"There's healing in His wings"
And because He rose we too shall rise.

"My God, My God, Why hast Thou forsaken Me"

Matthew 27:46

Pull back the curtain, let me see
A vision of Eternity
Of realms beyond mere Space and Time,
To where there is no paradigm ,
And all our questions solved,
Why do we seek for something more,
To open that illusive door
And unknown territories explore
Where conflicts are resolved?
God holds the Key to "WHY and HOW"
It is not given to us now,
Nor even to his Son in Death,
Who, with His near-last laboring breath
Asked for the reason WHY!

New language!

Cell phones for the celibate and Twitters for the twits.

The Blackberry's for Southerners for breakfast with their grits.

The U Tube is for those who go out, tubing on the lake

Like Surfing, it's a dangerous sport that puts your life at stake.

The Web is for the Spiders and the Mouse for feline pets.

Texting now has got kids hooked

They cannot spell, they don't read books

Abbreviations now we see

(All I can say is "OMG!")

What happened to our language? has it changed with no regrets.?

I guess I'm just too old for this! It's high time to retire.

So I'll Log off and then Log On, and throw it on the fire.

On New Year's Day ,the late King George V1 read this to
the British people .' I said to the Man who stood at he Gate
of the Year "Give me a light, that I may walk safely into he
unknown And He replied " Put your hand in Mine, that will
be to you better than a light and safer than a known way"

A Man stood at the entrance to a brand new year

I asked Him for a light to show the way and stay my fear,

And in a softened tone of voice

He said to me "You make your choice,

An earthly light. or put your hand in Mine.

I'll guide you through the unknown way

And when we reach th'Eternal Day

You'll find I AM the Light and I'M the Way.!"

PSALM 19:1-4

We believe the sun has risen, we see it in the skies,
But even when the clouds are there to veil it from our eyes,
The trees, the mountains & the sea are radiant with the light
That somehow penetrates the clouds & makes our pathway bright.

So God exists, we do not see Him in His beauty rare
But we see His creation, so we know that He is there.
His glory, so the Psalmist writes the heavens do declare,
The stars & planets sing for all the universe to hear.

In some mysterious way we've learned the language of the spheres..
It supersedes the intellect, evoking praise & prayers..
Some things our spirit understands & not the mind,
We knock, we ask, and after fervent seeking, then we find

The Gem that beggars definition, we just can't define
Experience that God alone can give, it is Divine!

PSALM 23 : 6

Five miles down the road was the Village fair
Three schoolboys said "Let us go there"
So one wrote a note to the Teacher which read
'Johnny is ill and has gone to bed'

The others wrote notes to their teachers and signed
Their Mothers' names, thinking noone would find
That they had skipped School and had spent the whole day
Just having fun,doing nothing but play,

They did this for a week and noone said a word,
They'd pulled off a prank then they suddenly heard
That someone had seen them and told one boy's dad.
So that 'put a crimp' in the fun that they'd had !

That Father confronted his boy at the table
And said someone saw him, & now was he able
To refute the claim that he'd been to the fair,
Played truant from School 'cause he'd taken a dare?

Well, he had to admit it and burst into tears
"I'll not do that again if school's on fifty years!"
Then he waited, the belt to feel –Dad's leather srap
Wielded with power across his bare back.

But Dad with the wisdom that parenthood brought
And with Christian principles that he'd been taught
Knew that God's goodness brings us into line,
Instead af a penalty or a big fine.

And so with compassion his Father bestowed
His watch on his son, because he well knows
That "Goodness and Mercy" keep us on the Track
That boy followed Jesus, and never looked back !

Psalm 37:4

"Delight thyself in the Lord and He shall give thee
the desires of thine heart"
God's not a heavenly Santa Claus, just loaded with the stuff
That WE desire and He will give until we've had enough.
He's not an ATM machine for our convenience
To whom we go when in a jam for dollars, pounds and pence!
He is a loving Father who will give us what we need.
If we 'delight in Him' He guarantees that we'll receive
Desires that HE plants within, and then, if we believe
He will fulfill them as they DID originate with Him.
If we receive the many things that our 'old nature' craves,
We'd be reduced to lesser men in fact we would be slaves.
Paul said "To whom ye yield yourselves as servants to obey
His servants ye are" and make no mistake,
that's nature's way..
Let Christ in you your heart renew, developing a thirst
For all that's pure and holy. desiring Jesus first.

Quality Time

"Quality time" needs "quantity time"
for something of worth to develop.

A year cannot be condensed to a day,
nor a moment an hour can envelop.

The butterfly doesn't emerge in a week.

A diamond is there for the one who will seek.

We're creatures of time and we want all things now

But wait on the Lord, and He'll show you how

To renew failing strength, and learn patience!

QUESTIONS.

Religion and Philosophy fall short to satisfy

Enquiring minds that ponder situations that defy

The 'doctrine' that all troubles are results of willful sin

And those who 'have it good' and don't experience suffering

Have lived a perfect life, and so deserve the state they're in!

These radicals are hiding 'neath a strong hermetic shield

And don't allow their minds to even contemplate or yield

To any other focus than what they learned in youth————

The primitive ideas that their convictions are the truth.!

The 3 good friends who really tried to comfort poor old Job

Sincerely gave opinions and tried in vain to probe

Into the mysteries of pain and found it had eluded

Their keen analysis of Job and they were just deluded.

Then God came in ! At last the Problem-Solver would endorse

The oratorical displays that they had set in course !

Then God, in all His wisdom put the 4 of them in place

But God did not say what they hoped, and tell the reason why

He simply told them HE IS GOD

And that should satisfy!

Romans 7 & 8

Create in us a hunger for all that's pure and good.
And give to us ability to do the things we should.
Unlike Saint Paul's experience in Romans chapter seven

When contrary to his will, he fails and has to be forgiven.
We need the power to graduate
From chapter seven to chapter eight
And live in victory!

"SAIL ON"

Those words, Columbus spoke to fearful men
Who n'er would cross the bound'ries to the sea.
Within the confines of Gibraltar's Straits
They sailed, and felt secure and very safe.

Two Herculian Pillars were erected
To safeguard Sailors & they were directed
To go no further into unknown seas,
"Ne plus ultra" that is the border/
"No more Beyond" that was the order!

Columbus was a fearless man
Whose faith was bold and strong
To trembling sailors, blanched with fear,
He said, "Sail on,,,sail on !"

Then on one dark and epic night
Columbus cried "I see a light!"
The dawning of a day!
Their 'wisdom',born of abject fear
Would limit them no more,

Into the light of dawn they peered
And saw a new world's shore!
O heed the lesson that is taught
It is with heavenly wisdom fraught,

"Launch out into the deep' and find
New things that boggle human minds,
Sail on,,, and on,,,in spite of storm,
Tho' hull is battered, sails are torn ,

Keep sailing to that Heavenly world
And get there with your flag unfurled!

SARAH LAUGHED

Sarah laughed, just twice, she laughed!
Well, so it says in Scripture.
I hope they're not the only times,
But they give us two pictures
The bitter laugh of unbelief (Genesis 18)
The joyful laugh of great relief (Genesis 21)

Rejuvenation had begun
Sarah started to look young!
Her silver hair now turning black,
Her drooping chin has now gone back!
A new light's in her eye!

She walks with graceful steady pace,
Now has a new glow on her face,
God gave her a complete face-lift
And body too, oh what a gift!
For this took years off her and him.
Behold a new life did begin,
And Sarah had a child!

A boy was born, a promised son
A son, for whom they'd, waited long.
And now he's here, be of good cheer,
For her reproach is gone!

Yes, her reproach has gone at last,
No wonder that she laughed and laughed!

"Seek the Lord while He may be found"

"Yea, if I make my bed in Hell" the psalmist said, "He's there!"
For nowhere are the limits of God's providential care.
And no one is beyond the pale of His redemptive plan
It is the will of God that He will rescue fallen man.

"A bruis-ed reed He will not break
Nor quench a smoking flax"
A seeking soul He'll surely find
Although he's drugged out of his mind
(For some, it DOES take that !

When reasoning and logic are suspended for a while.
That's when the wondrous grace of God will go the extra mile
And meet the sinner who repents ,no matter what his state
The mighty grace and love of God ,a new man will create.

This actually happened
A man went through no end of Eastern Religions looking for
peace and the meaning of life.
When he was high on drugs one day, he had
a phenomenal encounter with Jesus,
This was SO real that he was convicted of sin., repented and
became a true follower of Christ.

SINAI AND CALVARY

Ten Commandments God made known
By fiery Finger, etched in stone.
Then Moses saw a dreadful sight
As he descended from the height,
And cried aloud," Do I behold
a calf, and idol made of gold?" !
Then Moses threw those tablets down
And shattered them upon the ground.
The Laws of God just etched in stone
Could never for their sin atone,
Man cannot reach that elevation
For he needs emancipation.
God has more resources yet
And Sinai's demands were met
When Jesus won the victory
On the mount of CALVARY!

SIX Ft:; OF EARTH.

Day was dying in the west.
Oh how he longed to get some rest,
But, alas! there's far to run
'Ere night falls with setting sun.
He started out with great ambition
For he was in good condition,
He had entered many a race
And he could adjust his pace,
And reach the goal in time.
This Race was different, he was told
These fields were worth a mint of gold,
And if he ran around all seven,
At sunset, all fields would be given
To the one who came in first.

Here he comes, panting with thirst!
"I've won!" he said, and fell down dead!
His greed had taxed his strength too far,
And now, here comes the Funeral car,
He took his last ride in the Hearse
And only needs six Ft of earth!

St Paul .Eph:3.1
2.Tim 1:8
St Paul, now in a Roman Jail
An ag/ed man, grey haired and pale
Is feeling chilled in his dank cell
And dictates to someone to tell
His friend and brother, Timothy
That when he visits,(soon, he hopes)
That he will bring his cozy cloak
And bring the parchments too.
He loved to read and loved to write
And keep in touch though not in sight.
He loved the saints where're he went
And many years of life were spent
Encouraging them all.
A scholar to the end was he
His spiritual maturity
He shares with us today.
His time in prison was not lost.
We do not really know the cost
For him, with failing eyes, to scribe
Such wondrous truths we can imbibe
And so be edified.
A "Prisoner of Rome" was he?
Oh no. he said repeatedly
That he accepted everything
As from the Christ, his Lord and King.

THE ANGEL'S SONG

I had a strange experience when I was only seven,
I did not understand it then, but I heard songs from Heaven
My parents were awake; I heard their voices soft and low,
I called my Mother and I said "Turn off the Radio"
She said, "It isn't on, my girl you're dreaming probably"
Then with a word of knowledge that she obviously had
She added, "You heard Angels singing, welcoming Granddad!"
And that was New Year's Day way back in 1933
The years went by and I dismissed it from my memory.
Regarding it as childish dreams or even fantasy.
Then after thirty three long years I heard that Song again,
I woke and I rejoiced to hear that lovely Heavenly strain.
The song of Angels! Yes I recognized that sweet refrain
My Mother called me on the phone to say that
Nanny had gone Home,
'Twas obvious! I should have known!

THE CHOICE IS YOURS

There they are from dawn to dusk
People with a golfing lust,
Rain or shine, they're going to play
No matter if it IS Sunday!
Striped umbrellas deck the green
Rain-soaked Putters can be seen
Concentrating on the game
Oblivious to the pouring rain !
Now they put some of us to shame
Who say,"No Church, 'cause it might rain"
GET UP AN GO what ere betide,
You won't get wet, it's dry inside!!!

The Christian Life

My life is built on solid Rock, and not upon the sand,
In times of storm I know my house immovable will stand.
Foundations laid in childhood from the precepts of God's Word
Can stand the test and bear the weight, thus honoring the Lord.

It is a fact. life shakes us up, and takes us by surprise,
But we can grow in grace and our reactions can be wise.
A Christian doesn't fall apart or put the blame on God.
Remember Jesus was a Man and on this earth He trod.

And so He knows our frailties and the dangers on our way
But He's committed to mankind and promised He would stay
With every Blood-bought soul until that great and glorious Day
When He'll present perfected saints before the Throne and say'
"I see the travail of my soul
And I am satisfied
These souls who built upon the Rock
Have now been glorified!"

THE DAWN OF FREEDOM

On his soap-box platform the Marxian leader spouts
In Hyde Park Speakers' Corner where many-a- crack-pot shouts
This Lenin-Lover's holding forth on "Evils of our Day"
And argues that "The Dawn of Freedom's" coming soon this way,

Then turning to the growing crowd, wearied with world War two,
He says they'll have a better life 'neath Communistic Rule..
"You Sirs" he shouts as he points out two rag-a-muffin Bums,
"You will have a home Sirs, when The Dawn of Freedom comes!"

"Oh we don't want no fancy 'omes we're 'appy like we are"
"Well, you could have a wife and kids and even drive a car!"
The Speaker tried to tell them of a future full of fun,
One Rag-a-Muffin said that he would rather be a Bum.

"But listen!" cried the Speaker "Folks, you do not understand
That when The Dawn of Freedom comes, the ordinary man
Will live like Royalty, drink good wine and eat the finest steak."
The heckler was determined now his way of life to state

Said "I don't want your lousy steak I'm 'appy like I am
I goes each week to Welfare and I gets a tin o' spam"
By now, the Marxist, mad with rage was confident and bold
Yelled "WHEN THE DAWN OF FREEDOM COMES
YOU'LL DO AS YOU"RE BLOODY –WELL TOLD!"

That's a "quote"

I am covered !!

Life's Drama

The Scripture is the ink in which good writers dipped their pens,
We love suspense and drama, and how well the story ends:
Poor Cinderella rises from the ashes of the fire
And dons a robe and shining shoes; what beautiful attire!
And Sleeping Beauty wakens from her sleep of virtual death
To feel the long-awaited Prince's kiss of living breath!
The Law, so perfectly portrayed in Hugo's Javier
Does not allow for mercy ;(Val jean doesn't 'have a prayer')
But in the end, we read the stubborn arm of Justice gives
And grace and mercy won, and the repentant sinner lives!.

It seems there's only one great theme that never can grow pale,
Before this great eternal theme, all other drama trail,
It is Redemption's theme throughout the Book of Holy Writ
Of One who came to rescue us from out the miry pit.
He clothes us with the spotless robe of His own righteousness
Now we, for evermore with love and gratitude shall bless
The Author of the Drama, who with wisdom infinite,
Took all our willful acting that has put us in this plight
And somehow worked it in the play and made it turn out right!
We're waiting for that final scene when He comes on the Stage:
He'll take the bow from every knee, from sinner & from Sage,
And we'll acknowledge Him who is the Author of it all
And everything that He created, at His feet shall fall.

THE GARAGE SALE

Time marches on, and erstwhile antique treasure
To modern man brings no or little pleasure,
And so for paltry dollars things are sold — —
Ornaments once valued like pure gold..

People driving slowly by
Saw some things that caught the eye
Back they went now to explore
Jewelry and books galore.

There among some musty junk
In an old hand-painted trunk
Was a well-worn Book which read
"Holy Bible" ; Someone said

"Now that old Book is so well worn
And many pages have been torn
That I don't think it's worth a dime
Let's leave it there, and not waste time.

The lady took it to the desk
And asked "How much is this old text?"
"A BIBLE ?" said the man," My dear.
There's no price on it, that is clear!,

Just take it,
Read it,
Seek the Lord,

NO PRICE IS RIGHT FOR GOD'S GOOD WORD!"

THE GOLFER

The arrogant golfer with confident stride

Walked up to the tee box with obvious pride,

And seeing the green in the distance afar

Said "Oh this one's easy. I'll be under par-

One drive and one putt and she'll be in the cup,

Put the ball on the tee and I'll wrap this one up."

With speed and great form, he whiffed really hard

Blew the ball off the tee and it rolled just a yard!

He said to the Caddy ,"What terrible luck"

"Now Sir," said the Caddy, "One Hell of a putt"

"WHO'S MILKING WHOM?"

Kathryn was a Guernsey Cow; she grazed in Bovet's field
And daily he would milk her and find that she could yield
Enough to feed his family for she could fill a churn,
The Farmer then could sell what's left & then some money earn.

One day a Salesman came to see old Bovet in his barn,
He gave a demonstration and spun him such a yarn
That in the end the farmer bought not one, but two machines!
So he could spend more time at home,
and less with Miss Kathryn

The Salesman thought he'd done real well, and to himself said
"WOW"
And for 'down-payment' on the bill, the Salesman took the cow!

THE MODERN CHURCH

The stage replaced the pulpit; tell me, what replaced the Cross?
They say," We don't want symbols"
do they know what they have lost?

Guitars and drums, not organs, a chorus, not a Hymn
Tradition? that's old-fashioned; let's throw it to the wind!

The raucous music that we hear is loud, so very LOUD
And singers crooning through the mike exciting all the crowd.

A far cry from the days when Music was a Ministry,:
They now perform a 'special' or a 'number, seems to me

That Cain is still presenting to the Lord his sacrifice,
All dressed up cute and pretty so that folks will say" That's
nice"

But God rejects such 'gifts' from us and longs that we would give
A sacrifice of prayer and praise and for His glory live.

THE MYSTERY
(1 Peter 1:12 & Colossians 1:26)

Christ had to come through Adam's race, be born of human kind,

"Great God of Wonders" yet reduced to microscopic size!

The Holy Spirit activates the Virgin's promised Seed
And Christ , in her was fully formed, the Son of God indeed.
No wonder angels sang for Joy On that first Christmas morn,

For they had missed the Eternal Word, perhaps had been forlorn!

They did not know Redemption's plan,
'twas hidden from their eyes

Until they saw the Heavenly Babe reduced to human size.
The Mystery that was from the Angels temporarily hidden

Has unto us, in Christ the Savior of the world been given

"Whatever you do—"

Whatever it is that your hand finds to do
Get on with the job and the Lord will bless you.
A pen or a pencil, a needle and thread
Two willing hands that will make loaves of bread,

A shovel, a pick-axe, cement and a trowel
A basin of water, wash cloth and a towel,
Be faithful in small things, though humble they be
And you will bless others and find He'll bless thee!

It isn't success that we need to strive for,
It's just being faithful and true to the core,
Be sure that you work with the right driving force,
And make up your mind that you'll stay on the course

He'll bless what you write, what you sew, what you make.
And lead you the right way, for His own Name'sake

The Paraclete

This is a true story John Bunny told as an illustration
on how the Holy Spirit
Is the "One who comes along-side us"—
the Encourager the Paraclete!

With flagging strength and bated breath,

The runner thought he'd meet his death

But, win the marathon he must,

He could not lose his Coach's trust,

He'd learned so much about the race,

He had to keep a steady pace,

If he would reach the Goal.

Then suddenly his Coach emerged

From out the crowd, and in him surged

A powerful thrust, now win he must!

The Coach runs by his side!

///

We need not suffer sad defeat,

He's with us, Heaven's Paraclete!

THE PUZZLE

A Preacher was sitting alone at his desk
Searching the Script or a suitable text
He pondered a few, but he could not settle
Then in came his boy and he started to meddle
With books, pens and pencils & crayons galore
Until he had things strewn all over the floor.
The kid kept on chatting (Dad wished for a muzzle)
Then to his delight, on his desk saw a Puzzle—
A map of the world, so he thought , with a smile
'This will keep the kid busy and quiet for a while!"

* * * * * * * * * * *

But soon he was finished, the Puzzle completed.
The boy was excited as his Dad he greeted:
"I did it" he said, with his face all aglow,
"There's a man on the back of that Puzzle, you know~
So I got him right, now the world is right too",
The Preacher stopped searching and said ,
"Son, Thank you!"

The River of Grace Ezekiel 47:9

The River of God's Grace has flowed from all Eternity,
And from the Throne, Ezekiel saw it flowing full and free
'Twas hidden from the eyes of men until the time was right
Then in the town of Bethlehem the Shepherds saw the sight
Of Angels all rejoicing for they recognized the One
Whose Grace was there personified in God's beloved Son
Grace found the way to Egypt and to Nazareth we know,
And everywhere it went it carried blessings in its flow.
Through Nazareth & Bethany and then Gethsemane
And at the Crucifixion on the hill of Calvary
A dying thief repented as the River made its way
Up Calvary's Hill, & on his parch/ed lips he caught the Spray
Of grace abundant that would quench his thirst eternally
Then Jesus reassured him that in Paradise they'd be
It plunged into the depths below and quenched the fires of Hell
Then on to Philippi it flowed to flood a prison cell.
Then on and on the River flowed, now it is streaked with Blood
It gathered strength as on it went- a River now in flood!
'Gainst rocks of opposition then, the might waters hurled,
One stream flowed east, the other west and covered all the world!

* *

David Owen preached in Reading Berkshire U ,K in 1943 on this subject

The Simple Life

There's a 'gypsy-strain' in humanity, a constant moving on
We are dissatisfied with things we grasp, for then, they're gone!
Is anything fulfilling real desires that are deep?
Is all that Life can offer us a joy we cannot keep?
Well, Jesus has the answer to these questions of the heart,
Things do not give to us the joy He only can impart.
A person's life does not consist of things he can possess,
Like houses, lands and wealth and fancy fashionable dress.
There's something satisfying about 'sweet simplicity'
A humble home and modest fare, peace and tranquility.
"My peace" He said, "I'll give thee, that no one can take from thee"
It's not the peace and quiet of the Church's Cemetery!
It's a profoundly active force that culminates in joy,
It settles and it satisfies and somehow in that peace we find
Nomadic tendencies restrained,
A stabilizing peace regained
And that's simplicity.

THE SOLUTION

What silly excuses flustered people now give

For reckless behavior and life-styles they live!

You are so frustrated in 'finding yourself'

Don't search the world over, check your mental health.

I'm sorry, my friend, but I don't 'feel your pain!'

"Who am I?" you ask. WHAT? You do not know your name?

You are like the young boy who,'til he went to school

Thought his name was "Shutup" and his brother, "Youtoo"

You 're 'needing more space?

Think you're in a cocoon?'

I've got the solution—

TAKE OFF TO THE MOON!

The Whole Creation Groans

All Nature plays a Symphony in doleful minor key
And if we pause to listen it will give to you and me
A sense of interruptedness, where every cadence sounds
Imperfect and so incomplete,, but why should it astound
The person who has learned that Nature is beneath a curse?
And music's wrenched from dreams of a Utopia on Earth
Which is in process of a long drawn-out recovery
Awaiting the fulfillment of a Bible prophesy
Earth groans in travail, but we know the time will surely be
When minor chords will all resolve to brighter major key,
'Twill play again that first refrain – of Eden's ecstasy
As from the gate of Heaven comes the One who tunes the key
The whole Creation's groaning now, for that Eternal Day
When cadences will then resolve in Major harmony.

THE WORD.

O let me trace the sunbeam to the Sun,
As I receive the gift & thank the One
Whose hand so bountifully strew my path
With blessings mercy-laden that surpass
What I have ever dreamed or ever asked.

That under-statement, "God is good"
Is what we say and so we should.
Inadequate we find our speech,
We search in vain, and cannot reach
The adjective illusive.

It's not dawned upon the human mind
Nor tongue yet formed
A word for mortals to define.
The nearest we can say is "He's Divine"

God is Spirit, God is Love
Lion of Judah, yet a Dove!
The Root, the Branch of Jesse's rod
The Rose of Sharon in earth's sod!
God's so great, we can't describe
Neither can the Scriptures find
One single word and so God sends
His only Son, and John contends
HE is the WORD, hear Him .

John 1: 1

John 1:14

The Word was made flesh

And he came to express

The Image of God in perfection.

The Spirit's been sent

The Word to present

And to teach us His ways & direction (St John,16:13)

Christ did not write a book nor engrave on a stone

His will & His ways to make known,

But with power He endued

More than one hundred Jews (Acts 1:8)

The Gospel to take to the Nations.

THESE DAYS

We live with gadgets & machines
We talk to them and so it seems
No human beings hear the 'phone,
It answers us with "I'm not home,"

Great Grandma would turn in her grave
If she could see the time we save
With all of our electric; things
She'd ask "What do you do but binge?"

No sticks to chop, no soup to make,
No need to boil, no need to bake
It's all in cans and frozen pouches,
Microwave it, - no one grouches,

For they never tasted dinner
Like she made it-what a Winner-!
Ribbons & medallions won
At the "Bake-off" oh what fun!

No one could top Grandma's pie
For her secret, one must spy
As she makes it, trying hard
Not to show she's using LARD!

That's enough of Granny's days!
Don't get stuck in old set ways,
Times are changing, changing fast,
Nothing does for ever last.

I'm glad for all time-saving skills-
Betty Crocker, General Mills,
Food's good, frozen or in tins,
Make sure you get vitamins!

VISIT US AGAIN

Visit us again Oh lord, visit us again

Send, according to Thy Word

The showers of latter rain

O enlarge our habitation

Let us pray and toil

And the lord will send from Heaven

Corn and wine and Oil

We are waiting and expecting Thee indeed

Come Thou great El Shaddai & meet our need.

Let the young men now see visions,

Handmaids prophesy,

Lets obey the great commission

'As the day draws nigh

Visit this new generation

With a mighty shower

Let us see Thy great salvation

-Come in old-time power

We are waiting and expecting Thee indeed

Come Thou great El Shaddai and meet our need

We're missing it!

It isn't seminars or books or someone's bright idea,
It isn't any man-made thing, the Bible makes that clear.
We need a Sovereign Act of God to bring us back in line,
Revival like we've never known, for which we old folks pine.
We long to see the Holy Ghost fall on the Congregation,
And we shall hear the songs of praise as sinners find Salvation,
The singing 'in the Spirit' soars and echoes through the Choir,
They pick it up with great crescendos lift it even higher.
We used to hear the overtones: did Angels join the songs?
And if our eyes were opened would we've seen the Heavenly throng?

Lord, give us days again when our young men shall visions see,
And handmaids once again will give a word of prophesy.

Wells of Salvation

I will draw; I will drink from the wells of Salvation,

And sing "Praise the Lord, for there's no condemnation"

I am free! I'm forgiven; I'm going to Heaven,

I've been washed in the Blood of the Lamb!

Jesus died, and He rose for my justification,

He's seated in Heaven on His Throne,

And one glorious day, He will take me away

To the Place He's prepared for his own.

"Whatsoever a man soweth, that shall he also reap"

Everything is poisoned by the 'spirit of the age'
There's hardly any book today, but there on every page
You find the name of God in vain obscenities are spelled out plain
And Sit-coms?-'down the drain!

Too bad that in the last decade the standards have gone down
And values, held in high esteem are trampled on the ground.

Thank God that there is "Welfare" or those in dire need,
But many joined the' lazy ranks' and they, the System bleed.

Folks wonder if there'll be enough to pay their Pension Checks
Well, take the blame yourselves as the connection is direct-

Near sixty million babies were aborted years ago
Who would be paying taxes now, and coffers overflow.

Remember what the old folks said?
It's true, so very true————-
"You cannot have your cake and think that you can eat it too!"

"WHO AM I ?"

"Who am I?" is the latest craze,
The question puts me in a haze,
Please tell me what on earth they mean,
Their Birth Record have they not seen
And don't they know their name?

WE'RE people, all of us unique
In how we look and how we speak.
My DNA is mine alone
And God forbid they make a clone
And claim that she is me!

That would not be a person whole,
Made up of body mind and soul!
Now she might well ask who SHE is
And get herself into Show Biz
Then I'll claim royalties!

WONDER

I want to keep the wonder
That I knew when I was young,
The freshness of a morning,
As a new day had begun,
The smell of rain-freshed meadows,
And the beauty of the dew — — — — —
Scintillating rainbows of variegated hue
The wonder of a loaf of bread
Just rising in the heat
(I did not know about the action
Of the stuff called yeast!)
It seemed like magic to my mind
And everything that I could find
Evoked a sense of awe!
Let's keep a sense of wonder
Of our faculties and ponder
What life would be without ability
To smell, to taste. to see, to hear,
They all are gifts of God, that's clear.
"Great God of wonders", I exclaim,
"From Heaven's glory Jesus came,

And He's the greatest Wonder of them all."

INDEX

CPSIA information can be obtained at www.ICGtesting.com
Printed in the USA
BVOW10s1159131013

333586BV00003B/3/P